Henry Stephens Salt

Richard Jefferies. A study

Henry Stephens Salt

Richard Jefferies. A study

ISBN/EAN: 9783337732080

Printed in Europe, USA, Canada, Australia, Japan

Cover: Foto ©ninafisch / pixelio.de

More available books at **www.hansebooks.com**

BY
H. S. SALT

WITH A PORTRAIT

London
SWAN SONNENSCHEIN & CO.
NEW YORK: MACMILLAN & CO.
1894

CONTENTS

	PAGE
CHAPTER I.—AS MAN .	1
,, II.—AS NATURALIST .	31
,, III.—AS POET-NATURALIST	49
,, IV.—AS THINKER .	70
,, V.—AS WRITER .	96
BIBLIOGRAPHICAL APPENDIX .	121

PREFATORY NOTE

—>*<—

It must be premised that this little book is a study, not biography, of Richard Jefferies, though in the opening chapter I have indirectly related the chief circumstances of his life. For biographical details readers are referred to Mr. Besant's *Eulogy of Richard Jefferies*, and the later supplementary essays by Mr. P. Anderson Graham and Dr. R. Garnett.

I have embodied in the book, with the kind permission of the editors, the substance of articles contributed by me to *Temple Bar*, the *Pall Mall Gazette*, *To-day*, the *National Reformer*, etc. For information concerning the successive editions of Jefferies' works, and for leave to quote passages illustrative of his opinions and style, I am indebted to the courtesy of his publishers, Messrs. Smith, Elder & Co., Messrs. Longmans, Green & Co., Messrs. Chatto & Windus, Messrs. R. Bentley & Son, Messrs. Cassell & Co., and Messrs. Sampson Low & Co. I would further express my obligation, for assistance of various kinds to Dr. S. A. Jones, Mr. P. Anderson Graham, Dr. R. Garnett, and Mr. Arthur W. Nott.

The frontispiece portrait is reproduced from the only extant photograph of Jefferies, taken by the London Stereoscopic Company in 1879. The four illustrations of "Jefferies-land," which accompany the large-paper edition, were specially prepared for the purpose by Miss Bertha Newcombe.

RICHARD JEFFERIES.

I.—AS MAN.

It has been remarked by De Quincey, with profound psychological insight, that the thought of death is especially affecting in the summer, and that "any particular death haunts the mind more obstinately and besiegingly in that season," the "tropical redundancy of life" suggesting by very contrast the "frozen sterilities of the grave." True in general, this saying finds a peculiar and pathetic illustration in the case of Richard Jefferies, whose untimely death can scarcely fail to be associated and contrasted, in the minds of those who love his personality and writings, with that "Pageant of Summer" which he so wonderfully and feelingly depicted. For Jefferies, above all other writers, was the high priest of summer; his warm, sensuous, southern nature breathed intense reverence for the "alchemic, intangible, mysterious power, which cannot be supplied in any other form but the sun's rays." Who else could have described, as he has described, the glare, the glamour, the multitudinous hum, the immense prodigality of a high summer noon? The "great sun burning in the heaven" is the burden and inspiration not only of the autobiographical *Story of my Heart*, but of all the most imaginative outpourings of his fervent spirit, which was destined too soon, alas, to be quenched in that wintry darkness which it so surely and instinctively foreboded.

This lavish ardour of temperament, which regarded every form of asceticism as "the vilest blasphemy," and in its insatiable yearning for a full, rich life, chafed against the niggardliness of time and destiny, must be kept well in view by all readers who would understand the meaning of Jefferies' career. It is furthermore a noticeable fact that all his memorable work was produced within a compass of ten years, of which no less than six were years of increasing illness and debility. The pathos of this contrast between the ideal and the actual, between triumphant aspiration and crushing disappointment, has left a strong mark on his writings; he is at once confident and despondent—despondent in the failure of the present and the past, confident in the belief that the human race will hereafter realise the utmost dreams of his ambition.

The story of Richard Jefferies is that of a man who, not without many misgivings and errors and difficulties, outgrows at last—if indeed he ever wholly outgrows—the littlenesses and vulgarities of local environment, and the mere personal ambitions of his own lower self. He was not one of those highly-favoured mortals who spring forward at once to some congenial life-work, in confident and single-hearted recognition of an appointed task; on the contrary, his early years are mostly a record of ill-conceived hopes and painful though inevitable disillusionment. The descendant of an old stock of Wiltshire yeomen, which had long transmitted from generation to generation the native tendency to a proud reserve and distrustful solitude, he was born into this family (November 6th, 1848) at a time when circumstances and misfortunes had accentuated its distinguishing character. The ancestral farm-house at Coate, for all the picturesqueness of its position and surroundings, was then under the shadow of approaching ruin, and the small property, which had already been twice lost and twice recovered by the Jefferies' family, was soon to pass altogether into other hands.

In his father, the "Farmer Iden" of *Amaryllis at the Fair*, the boy saw exemplified in the fullest degree those conflicting traits which he himself in no small measure inherited—the dignity derived from high natural gifts and great accumulated knowledge, side by side with the utter incapacity to turn such powers to any practical account. Here was a man of noble presence, in whose forehead "there was too much thought for the circumstances of his life"; a man whose fortune was ever steadily on the decline, though he would bring to the planting of "a few paltry potatoes" an infinitude of patient science and skill. "What a fallacy it is," exclaims the son, who in his *Amaryllis at the Fair* has left what is undoubtedly a transcript from his own early experiences, "that hard work is the making of money; I could show you plenty of men who have worked the whole of their lives as hard as ever could possibly be, and who are still as far off independence as when they began."

The country which lies around Coate, a country of rich grassy lowlands dominated by high, bare downs, is one which is full of treasure for naturalist and archæologist alike; in no other district, perhaps, could the future writer of *Wild Life in a Southern County* have found choicer material for his work. All the best characteristics of typical English scenery were grouped within easy distance of Richard Jefferies' birthplace. About a hundred yards from the house is Coate lake, or reservoir, a large sheet of water which played an important part in the canoe voyages and other adventures of his childhood, and is frequently referred to in his writings.[1] But it was the Downs in particular that influenced his youthful imagination; and we are informed, on the authority of one who learned it from Jefferies himself, that "it was when he roamed about the long, rolling Downs that he felt his life most full, his thoughts most clear, his spirit most exalted and yet most at rest."[2]

For the present, it is sufficient to notice that from his earliest years this bitter contrast was forced on Jefferies' observation—on the one hand the opulence of nature in the wild, free life of bird and beast and

---

[1] *E.G.*, in *Bevis* and *After London*. The Reservoir is now, like Walden Pond, frequented by tourists and holiday-makers.

[2] Frederick Greenwood, *National Observer*, August 2nd, 1890.

flower, and the corresponding fulness of human knowledge and endeavour—on the other, the narrowing pressure of personal isolation and pecuniary embarrassment. By his father, the quiet, thoughtful, peasant philosopher, who would expatiate, now in broadest Wiltshire dialect, now in purest English, on the birds and trees and flowers which he knew so well, he was early initiated into those mysteries of wood-craft and nature-lore wherein he, too, was destined to become so great a master; from his father he part inherited, part learned, the habit of moody independence and self-centred judgment, which lent a mingled strength and weakness to his character. In this way the paternal influence was strong, yet from the first the boy seems to have lacked for true human friendship. He had no intimate confidences except with wild nature, his books, and his own soul.

The eldest surviving child of a family of five, he had for his daily playmate a brother one year younger than himself, but neither with him nor with the other country boys of his native village was he ever closely in sympathy. "This unbending independence and pride of spirit," thus he writes of himself, under the name of Felix, in *After London*, "together with scarce-concealed contempt for others, had resulted in almost isolating him from the youth of his own age, and had caused him to be regarded with dislike by his elders. He was rarely, if ever, asked to join the chase, and still more rarely invited to the festivities and amusements provided in adjacent houses. . . . Between the two brothers there was the strangest mixture of affection and repulsion. The elder smiled at the excitement and energy of the younger; the younger openly despised the studious habits and solitary life of the elder. In time of real trouble and difficulty they would have been drawn together; as it was, there was little communion; the one went his way, and the other his."

These solitary habits, at first neither encouraged nor repressed by his parents, were at last in some sort acknowledged. "One of the upper rooms of the farm-house," says Mr. Besant—"the other was the cheese-room—was set apart for him alone. Here he had his books, his table, his desk, and his bed. This room was sacred. Here he read; here he spent all his leisure time in reading. He read during this period an immense quantity. Shakespeare, Chaucer, Scott, Byron, Dryden, Voltaire, Goethe—he was never tired of reading *Faust*—and it is said, but I think it must have been in translation,[1] that he read most of the Greek and Latin masters." To the quietude of that room next the cheese-room we are perhaps indebted for some of the most splendid products of Jefferies' after genius.

Indeed he seems to have been more fortunate in this respect, and to have owed more to his father's example, than has been generally recognised. Here is the testimony of Mr. Charles Jefferies, one of his younger brothers.[2]

---

[1] There is no doubt on this point. See the essay on "Nature and Books" in *Field and Hedgerow*, p. 34. "I read them in English first, and intend to do so to the end."

[2] *Pall Mall Gazette*, September 22nd, 1891, "An Interview with Jefferies' brother."

"Our parents were related to some London publishers who regularly stocked us with all sorts of books, while my father always manifested a love of reading, which he early instilled into us as boys. His favourite volumes were the Bible and Shakespeare, and alternately he regularly read to us from their pages, explaining and elucidating as he went on. Richard early in life emulated my father's pleasure in reading. His acquaintance with the good old Book was very extensive, and it was difficult for anyone to puzzle him with questions concerning it."

But the young student, if report may be trusted, did not rely wholly on his London relatives for his supply of literature. In a passage of his early novel, *World's End*,[1] which has all the appearance of being autobiographical, he describes how the youthful hero —presumably the "Amateur Poacher" of a later volume—used to trap hares and rabbits, and sell them to some friendly carriers, who in exchange supplied him with books, and how the books after being read were re-sold through the same agents at half price. The following sentences have a special interest, not only as throwing light on Jefferies' early studies, but as anticipating in some degree what is so rarely foreshadowed in his juvenile writings—the tone and manner of his mature style.

"He bought also most of the English poets, a few historians, and a large number of scientific works, for he was devoured with an eager curiosity to understand the stars that shone so brilliantly upon those hills— the phenomena of Nature with which he was brought

---

[1] Vol. ii., p. 12.

in daily contact. . . . He saw, he felt Nature. The wind that whistled through the grass, and sighed in the tops of the dark fir trees, spoke to him a mystic language. The great sun in unclouded splendour slowly passing over the wide endless hills, told him a part of the secret. His books were not read, in the common sense of the term; they were *thought* through. Not a sentence but what was thought over, examined, and its full meaning grasped and firmly implanted on the memory." [1]

As with his immediate friends and acquaintances, so too was his relationship with the neighbours of the Coate hamlet affected by his love of seclusion. "Was everyone then so pleasant to me in those days?" he exclaims in one of his latest reminiscences.[2] "Were the people all so beneficent and kindly that I must needs look back; all welcoming with open hand and open door? No, the reverse; there was not a single one friendly to me. . . . No one else seems to have seen the sparkle on the brook, or heard the music at the hatch, or to have felt back through the centuries; and when I try to describe these things to them they look at me with stolid incredulity."

There is, indeed, good reason to believe that the Jefferies' household, so strange and so unsociable in its habits, was regarded by the neighbours with genuine, if not altogether friendly amazement. Not the least surprising figure to the simple village folk was that of Richard Jefferies himself, as he grew up into the tall, lank, shambling youth, indifferent to all considerations

---

[1] *World's End*, ii., 12, 13.
[2] "My Old Village," *Field and Hedgerow*.

of dress and appearance—the "Belgian Lamp-post," as the humour of the country-side laboriously nicknamed him after his return from an adventurous but ill-starred visit to the Continent. For exactly as the youthful Thoreau aroused the virtuous astonishment of his busy fellow-citizens at Concord, when instead of adopting some respectable and remunerative profession he devoted himself to his out-door calling as "self-appointed inspector of snowstorms and rain-storms," so the sight of the rambling meditative Jefferies was doubtless a sore trial and perplexity to the worthy Wiltshire yeomen. Let me here quote the authority of some very interesting remarks on Jefferies' early life.[1]

"The son of poor parents, be he ambitious or contented, lazy or energetic, finds it necessary at an early age to do something for his living, and the shrewd country-folk hastened Jefferies to a decision by showing a certain contempt for his agricultural accomplishments. Long after his name was famous as a writer, the be-smocked village patriarch remembers him as 'nowt o' a farmer' and 'a lazy lout on the land'; and there was one who used to tell with pride how he had openly rebuked the indolent loafer. . . . 'See'd ye owt on the Downs?' one would ask, as dusk was settling down on the grey hills, and 'Nobbut Dick Jefferies moonin' about' would be replied. Some thought him incorrigibly lazy, and told him so; others reckoned him half-cracked, and pitied his family."

Such judgments are only what must be anticipated and calculated for by men of Jefferies' temperament.

---
[1] P. Anderson Graham. *Nature in Books*, p. 13, 14.

Indeed the naturalist or nature student is everywhere looked upon by the generality of country-folk as a lunatic at large (except, of course, in those lucid intervals when he is engaged in "killing something," an operation which for the time rehabilitates him in the popular interest and esteem), and if this is the common verdict even on the well-to-do gentlemen who have money and leisure at their command, far sterner is the local censure when the delinquent is some raw youth who has ventured to desert the honoured temple of Mammon for no more serious purpose than to frequent the neglected temple of Nature.

There was, however, this important difference between Thoreau's case and Jefferies', that whereas the Concord transcendentalist betook himself deliberately and of set purpose to the life-long pursuit of his ideal, the young Wiltshire yeoman was wholly unaware of the momentous influence which these early nature studies were already exercising on his character and were eventually to exercise on his life—nay, more, he was under the quite intelligible, but in his case erroneous, impression, that his real purpose in the world, like that of ordinary people, was to "get on," to make money, to jostle and scramble for a livelihood along the well-worn paths of competition. While fully recognising that no reproach is due to Jefferies on this account, but rather the contrary, since he showed as much diligence and determination with the pen as the most industrious of his ancestors with the spade, I think all readers of the history of his early manhood, and of the passages from his letters quoted or summarised by his biographer, must have been struck by the extremely commonplace, not to say vulgar character of his interests and aspirations.

The need of money-making was from the very first his bane. Left without the guiding advice or assistance which a young man might reasonably have expected from his father, but at the same time enjoying the compensating advantage of perfect freedom in his plans, he adopted the journalistic profession as the readiest method of earning an adequate remuneration for his work, without altogether chaining himself as a wage-slave to the desk. It was, however, romanticism, not journalism, that he had ultimately in view; and it is evident enough that his professional duties as reporter to a local Wiltshire paper were not very congenial to him. We are told that "he never made himself a proficient, far less an adept, at writing shorthand; he never learnt more than barely sufficed for ordinary work."[1] In the first volume published by him, an obscure little treatise on *Reporting, Editing, and Authorship* (1872), he cynically states his opinion that "it is better at once to realise the fact, however unpleasant it may be to the taste, and instead of trying to win the goodwill of the public by laborious work, treat literature as a trade, which, like other trades, requires an immense amount of advertising."

Jefferies' futile attempts to advertise his own youthful writings were indicative of an unreasonably sanguine temperament—a characteristic hopefulness which was

[1] P. Anderson Graham.

gradually replaced by a still more rooted despondency. During the first ten or twelve years of his literary apprenticeship he produced a succession of quite worthless novels, culminating in 1874 with that fearful and wonderful production *The Scarlet Shawl* (a book which surely sounds the lowest depths of dulness and inanity), and in spite of many well-merited rebuffs he persisted almost to the end in the delusion that he possessed the requisite qualities of a novelist. His mixture of simplicity and worldliness is pathetic in its absurdity. He sends some boyish verses to the Prince Imperial, and hails a very ordinary acknowledgment as "a wonderful recommendation." He consults Disraeli about finding a publisher for a novel, and sees "a guarantee of success" in the politely evasive answer of that astute statesman. So great is his fatuity that even a publisher's stereotyped assurance of "full consideration"—that too frequent precursor of the fatal "declined with thanks"—is welcomed by him as "a very promising phrase." The whole outward record of this period of his life is a dull and sordid and depressing one; a certain dogged though misdirected industry is the only relieving feature, and even this industry tends to deepen the ultimate sense of defeat. "You have no idea," he writes in 1873, "of the wretched feeling produced by incessant disappointment, and the long long months of weary waiting for decisions without the least hope."

It may well be that much of this failure was due to the fact that the education which Jefferies received was very inadequate to his capacities. Looking back on his career as a whole, and regarding him now as a well-known literary figure, we are apt to forget that he was but a self-educated countryman, and that he inherited the disabilities no less than the advantages of his position. "Thus then," says his biographer, "the boy was born, in an ancient farmhouse beautiful to look upon, with beautiful fields and gardens round it, in the midst of a most singular and interesting country, wilder than any other part of England except the Peak and Dartmoor, encouraged by his father to observe and remember, taught by him to read the Book of Nature. What better beginning could the boy have had? There wanted but one thing to complete his happiness—a little more ease as regards money."

But the circumstances of Jefferies' lot were such that the want of money meant the want of any ease whatever. Proud, sensitive, reserved, resentful, he was largely deficient in the cultured judgment and self-balance which result from a liberal training, and are among the chief passports to success. A nature such as this was altogether out of place in the ordinary struggle for promotion; and herein we must seek the explanation of the many false starts made by Jefferies in the early part of his career, so deformed, externally at least, by a crude sentimentality and a complete absence of humour. It was with him as with Byron's hero:

> "And one by one in turn, some grand mistake
> Casts off its bright skin yearly, like the snake."

I have said that the external record of Jefferies' early life is one of sordid mediocrity; I would not for a moment be understood to imply that his true inner life is liable to any such disparagement. Nothing is more instructive than to note how the genius, the vital part of the man, at first dormant and inactive, was gradually developing and asserting itself, and how, under all the superficial commonplaceness of his struggle for professional advancement, the spirit of the real, the disinterested Jefferies was preserved clear and inviolable. So little did he understand himself that he never suspected in these early years where his best strength lay; and when, after his marriage, in 1874, to the daughter of a neighbour at Coate, he left his native hamlet to seek a living in the world, he little foresaw that the memory of the very scenes he was leaving would furnish him with the best material of his after-work. The problem of his career was so simple that for a time he wholly missed its solution. Here, in truth, the stone which the builders rejected was to become the headstone of the corner—Nature, the study which of all studies was nearest and dearest to him, was forgotten in his eagerness to "get on," yet the knowledge was already accumulated in his mind, and the passion was latent there also, needing but a touch to call it forth.

From his father, and from a friendly gamekeeper whom he was privileged to accompany on his rounds, he had acquired a very full and exact acquaintance with the fauna and flora of the neighbourhood; he was a naturalist, without being aware of it, while he was yet a boy. In this there was perhaps nothing very uncommon, except that in Jefferies' case the knowledge gained by him had been stamped on his mind, as was afterwards made evident, with extraordinary clearness and precision.

But far more important that this hereditary woodcraft were the novel and unfamiliar experiences which he was already learning *from himself*—the passionate and mystic communion with Nature, that gave him an insight into depths which the mere "naturalist" can never fathom. "I was not more than eighteen," he says,[1] "when an inner and esoteric meaning began to come to me from all the visible universe, and indefinable aspirations filled me. I found them in the grass fields, under the trees, on the hill-tops, at sunrise, and in the night. There was a deeper meaning everywhere. The sun burned with it; the broad front of morning beamed with it; a deep feeling entered me while gazing at the sky in the azure noon, and in the starlit evening."

These and other personal details are recorded in that characteristic and remarkable volume, *The Story of my Heart, my Autobiography* (1883), a title which is fully justified by the contents, although there is in the book but little narrative of facts and dates and places. Real autobiographies — autobiographies in which the writer unveils not the outward circumstances of his fortunes and life, but the inner intellectual and spiritual history of himself—are rare indeed, and this is one of them. It is just for this reason, because it

---

[1] *The Story of my Heart*, p. 199.

is the story of a heart and not of a lay-figure, that it possesses a peculiar and inexpressible charm for some readers, especially, of course, for those who are in accord with the main current of Jefferies' thoughts and aspirations.

I am aware that the literal truth of such reminiscences must be accepted with a certain amount of caution; for, as one of the most sagacious of Jefferies' critics has aptly remarked, " They are hardly what the lad really thought, but embody all he was to think when he should have come intellectually to man's estate."[1] Nevertheless, I regard these autobiographical passages as substantially trustworthy, and of the utmost importance to the student of Jefferies' works, for it was just this germ of higher thought and spiritual absorption in Nature which was able to redeem his character and genius from the trammels of a worldly preoccupation. That the youth who was ostensibly engaged in the materialistic pursuits of journalism should be the recipient from time to time of these spiritual intimations, is a sufficient clue to the tenor of his subsequent career.

The several steps by which Jefferies was led to the discovery of his distinctive faculty and to the realising of his hopes appear clearly in his narrative. In 1872, two years before his marriage, while he was working as a reporter at Swindon, from which town Coate is only two miles distant, and vainly sending his worthless juvenile novels the round of the London publishing-houses, he scored his first success

---

[1] Dr. Garnett, in *National Dictionary of Biography*.

by three letters which he contributed to the *Times* on the subject of "The Wiltshire Labourer." This doubtless suggested to him that to write on agricultural matters, of which (however prejudiced his standpoint [1]) he had a direct personal knowledge, was at least as rational a way of exercising his literary skill as to compose sentimental romances concerning scenes of which he knew nothing. Accordingly, during the next few years, though the novel-writing still continued, we find him producing a number of essays, mostly published in *Fraser's Magazine*, on "The Future of Farming," "Village Organisation," and other kindred topics of a more or less practical character. Thence, by an easy transition, he passed to descriptive and artistic work, as in the two early papers on "Marlborough Forest" and "Village Churches"; and this in turn led to the series of volumes beginning with *The Gamekeeper at Home*, by which his fame was permanently established.

His mature authorship dates from the commencement of his five years' residence at Surbiton, to which place he came in 1877 in order to be nearer London, while yet preserving what was to him a necessity of existence—a secure foothold in the country. This Surbiton period was a most important one in Jefferies' career, not so much because it provided material for those notable essays which are comprised under the title of *Nature near London*, as because it marked his progression from journalism to literature, from observation to thought. Coate, it is true, was still to

---

[1] See p. 81.

be the background of his finest word-pictures; but the influence of London was very powerful in quickening and humanising his imagination, for now for the first time he saw the poetry that is in the great city as well as the poetry that is in the open fields, and was able to ponder deeply and fervently on the vast social problems of his time. It is no mere paradox to say that he learnt the message of the country by coming to the town. The true significance of Nature, in its bearing on human destiny, was now gradually unfolded to him; and what had before been crude knowledge was now ripened into wisdom.

His whole status as a writer was revolutionised by this change. Henceforth no more sentimental romances or obsequious histories of the Goddards,[1] no more complimentary verses to princes, or touting letters to politicians; for Jefferies was now on the firm ground of his intimate knowledge of Nature, the one theme which he had not handled for self-advancement, and by which he was not in the end to be disillusioned and disappointed. Well might he say, as he afterwards said, "From the littleness and meanness and niggardliness forced upon us by circumstances, what a relief to turn aside to the exceeding plenty of Nature."

But the supreme step yet remained to be taken, the passage from mere artistic description to the higher forms of feeling, and to the full development and expression of that mystic nature worship which had

---

[1] *A Memoir of the Goddards of North Wilts*, Coate, Swindon, 1873.

been revealed to him by glimpses in his youth. It was from Nature and his own natural intuitions that he won the secret of his freedom. The false methods of conventionality had now to be painfully cast aside; it was his task "to unlearn the first ideas of history, of science, of social institutions; to unlearn one's own life and purpose; to unlearn the old mode of thought and way of arriving at things; to take off peel after peel, and so get by degrees slowly towards the truth." Then at length Jefferies attained, or well-nigh attained—for even in his latest writings there are signs that the lower self was never wholly subjugated—to a real philosophy of life, a possession not only of literary craftsmanship, but of intellectual and spiritual mastery. He was no longer a mere literary naturalist; he was an enthusiast, an idealist, and a thinker.

What Thoreau wrote of himself in his quaint epigrammatic stanzas might with equal truth be put into the mouth of Jefferies:—

"But now there comes unsought, unseen,
  Some clear divine electuary,
And I, who had but sensual been,
  Grow sensible, and as God is, am wary.

"I hearing get who had but ears,
  And sight who had but eyes before,
I moments live who lived but years,
  And truth discern who knew but learning's lore.

"I hear beyond the range of sound,
  I see beyond the range of sight,
New earths and skies and seas around,
  And in my day the sun doth pale his light."

But before this point was reached (for I have somewhat anticipated the crowning phase of his career), circumstance, that constant and implacable enemy of Jefferies' genius, was once more in the ascendant, and the nature-ideal which had with such difficulty worked itself clear of the depressing actualities of his early life, was yet to be thwarted and obscured by a long train of unforeseen and irreparable misfortunes. One would be disposed to marvel at the strange irony of fate whereby both Thoreau and Jefferies, the two men perhaps who, above all others, drew the most intense and vivid enjoyment from the simple fact of existence, were struck down in their prime and debarred from their intimate communion with wild nature, did we not know that they were both the victims of inherited physical weakness, and that such health as they temporarily enjoyed was due far more to their own indomitable spirit than to any vigour of constitution. "Our bodies," said Jefferies with a terrible significance of personal no less than general application, "are full of unsuspected flaws, handed down it may be for thousands of years, and it is of these that we die, and not of natural decay. . . . The truth is, we die through our ancestors; we are murdered by our ancestors. Their dead hands stretch forth from the tomb and drag us down to their mouldering bones."

The extreme vivacity of Jefferies' physical senses is made abundantly evident, not only from his own testimony, but indirectly from numberless passages in his writings which could only have been conceived by one who thirsted for beauty with all the thirst of "the sun-heated sands dry for the tide." "To me," he says, "colour is a sort of food; every spot of colour is a drop of wine to the spirit;" and elsewhere, "Colour and form and light are as magic to me; it is a trance; it requires a language of ideas to convey it."

"Out of doors, colours do not need to be gaudy—a mere dull stake of wood thrust in the ground often stands out sharper than the pink flashes of the French studio; a faggot, the outline of a leaf, low tints without reflecting power strike the eye as a bell the ear. To me they are intensely clear, and the clearer the greater the pleasure. It is often too great, for it takes me away from solid pursuits merely to receive the impression, as water is still to reflect the trees. To me it is very painful when illness blots the definition of out-door things—so wearisome not to see them rightly, and more oppressive than actual pain. I feel as if I was struggling to wake up with dim, half-opened lids, and heavy mind."[1]

We can judge from such passages how great was the loss which Jefferies must necessarily have endured when he was shut off from his deepest sources of inspiration; it is also fully evident that his bodily strength was at no time commensurate with his intellectual ambitions. His personal appearance and general mode of life were those of a man whose inherited slightness of constitution was only compensated by an unusual energy of will; indeed, it is probable, as Mr. Besant suggests, that "the consciousness of

---

[1] *The Open Air*, essay on "Wild Flowers."

physical weakness, the sense of impending early death, caused him to yearn with so much longing after physical perfection, and the fuller life which he clearly saw was possible." One of those who knew him personally has graphically described in some very interesting reminiscences the natural indolence of temperament which showed itself in his movements and manners.[1]

"It was to be seen in every look of him, in his build, in his gait, and even more when he moved across a room than when he sat in repose. 'Long' and 'lounge' have much the same meaning at the root, and Jefferies' length, to which every feature contributed, was languid and loitering to a marked degree. He was a long man from head to foot: his legs long, his arms long, his hands, his head, and the features of his face with its somewhat drooping eyelids and softly drooping mouth."

Here is the account of Jefferies' appearance as given by his biographer.

"In appearance Richard Jefferies was very tall—over six feet. He was always thin. At the age of seventeen his friends feared that he would go into a decline, which was happily averted—perhaps through his love for the open air. His hair was dark-brown; his beard was brown, with a shade of auburn; his forehead both high and broad; his features strongly marked; his nose long, clear, and straight; his lower lip thick; his eyebrows distinguished by the meditative droop; his complexion was fair, with very little

---

[1] "Richard Jefferies," by Frederick Greenwood, *National Observer*, August 2, 1890.

colour. The most remarkable feature in his face was his large and clear blue eye; it was so full that it ought to have been short-sighted, yet his sight was far as well as keen. His face was full of thought; he walked with somewhat noiseless tread and a rapid stride."

On the subject of Jefferies' physical powers, his own statement may be appropriately cited: "My frame could never take the violent exertion my heart demanded. Labour of body was like meat and drink to me. Over the open hills, up the steep ascents, mile after mile, there was deep enjoyment in the long-drawn breath, the spring of the foot, in the act of rapid movement. Never have I had enough of it; I wearied long before I was satisfied, and weariness did not bring a cessation of desire; the thirst was still there."[1]

Jefferies had been living for four years at Surbiton when his illness began in 1881, and from that time to the end in 1887, his life was a constant series of sufferings, to which neither medical advice nor surgical operations could bring any permanent relief. "I have tried," he says in *Amaryllis*, "the effect of forty prescriptions upon my person. With the various combinations, patent medicines, and so forth, the total would, I verily believe, reach eighty drugs." "Everything possible," says his biographer, "of long-continued torture, necessity of work, poverty, anxiety, and hope of recovery continually deferred, is crammed into the miserable record." During this period he

---

[1] *The Story of my Heart.*

several times changed his residence on account of his failing health, and lived successively at West Brighton, Eltham, Crowborough, and Goring, a village on the Sussex coast.

The disease was discovered to be an ulceration of the small intestine. The details of the illness (Jefferies was a most nervous and intractable patient) are so harrowing in their intensity that his biographer "dared not quote the whole of this dreadful story of long-continued agony," and gives extracts only from the letters addressed by Jefferies to a friend. Here he describes himself "as the veriest shadow of a man," and like a living man tied to a dead one, "mind alive and body dead." "Whatever I wish to do," he says, "it seems as if a voice said, No, you shall not do it; feebleness forbids. I think I should like a good walk. No. I think I should like to write. No. I think I should like to rest. No. Always No to everything."

And now we come to the most marvellous fact of all in Jefferies' life-story, the last terrible struggle of spiritual vigour against physical decrepitude. It was under these circumstances, or scarcely less afflicting than these, that he wrote the very best, and most characteristic, and most enduring of his essays, such as the triumphant "Pageant of Summer" or the immortal *Story of my Heart*, works which are unsurpassed as prose poems by anything which the English language contains. Shall we say that he produced these intellectual masterpieces wholly and absolutely *in despite of* his physical sufferings? or was there rather some subtle connection and interdependence between the conditions and the result? On this difficult but important question of psychology, I am glad to be able to quote from some highly interesting and suggestive *Notes on Richard Jefferies*, the manuscript of which has been kindly placed at my disposal by the author,[1] a well-known student of Thoreau.

"In studying the writings of Richard Jefferies it is necessary to consider his physical condition. He almost equalled Heine in suffering, and the probable nature of his diseases suggests the soil in which genius appears chiefly to flourish. His portrait indicates the scrofulous diathesis with its singularly impressionable temperament, its rapturous enjoyment of a delight and its intense susceptibility to a pang. In such an one the physical life is largely pathological; it is not to be estimated by the ordinary standard of the robust man.

"One of Jefferies' medical attendants said of him, 'He strikes me as being a marked example of hysteria in man, though in his case, as in many women, the commoner phenomena of hysteria are wanting.' This element in the diagnosis of Jefferies' mental condition is fully in accord with the teachings of modern medical science, but this same 'science' would find in the bloody sweat of Gethsemane only corpuscles, clot, and chloride of sodium, and to the latest date it is utterly unable to find any trace of the soul in the *caput mortuum* of its destructive analyses. This should be remembered, because there is a reproach in the ascription of 'hysteria' that is keenly felt by the subject. To the most recondite of the medical profession, be it known, hysteria is a mysterious supersensuous

---

[1] Samuel A. Jones, M.D., of Michigan University, U.S.A.

enigma; not even in catalepsy is the domination of mind over matter more strikingly manifested.

"If, then, Jefferies was a 'marked example of hysteria,' that is only saying in effect that he is one of those in whom is displayed the astounding mastery of the spiritual over the mere material; and whilst the essential nature of hysteria is unknown, its results are often as impressive as they are inexplicable. It was hysteria that made Joan of Arc a terror to the bravest of England's soldiery, and it was hysteria that nerved the arm of Luther when he threw his inkstand at the devil. If hysteria has its debasements, it has also its exaltations; if it can sink one unhappy subject as low as the brute, it can elevate another until his serene altitude is only 'a little lower than the angels.' Hysteria was doubtless called demoniac possession in the days of Jesus, but even in those days it was again hysteria that bestowed the gift of tongues, and brought the vision that blinded Saul of Tarsus while it illumined his soul.

"It was, then, a similar aberration from the orbit of the commonplace that gave Jefferies the heavenly glimpses which he vainly endeavours to describe in *The Story of my Heart*. There was one apocalypse on the island of Patmos, and another on that silent hill-top in Wiltshire; and to us both are alike incomprehensible. We who are not allowed these heavenly visions doubt the testimony of the beholder just as the tales of the early travellers were scoffed at by stay-at-home folk, whose only migrations were like those of Goldsmith's good vicar—'from the blue bed to the brown.'"

It is much to be regretted that we have no first-hand description of Jefferies' personality from one of the few friends who knew him intimately; for in the absence of full information there must necessarily be a certain element of conjecture in all such estimates of his character as that which I have quoted, though we may feel sure that the general conclusion is correct. But Jefferies, as we have seen, was a man of few confidences, and his constitutional reserve appears to have been intensified by suffering and disappointment as the years went on, until to a superficial observer he gave the impression of being even misanthropical and morose, though no sympathetic reader who has felt the heart-beats that throb through his impassioned *Story* could for a moment doubt the deep tenderness that inspired them.

His inability to make friendships is glanced at in an odd passage in one of his own volumes. "Has anyone," he says, "thought for an instant upon the extreme difficulty of knowing a person? Acquaintance is often difficult enough to acquire; to really come to know a stranger, a comparative stranger, is most difficult."[1] I have heard it humorously but pertinently suggested by a careful student of Jefferies' writings, that the one and only friendship made by him was with "the man in the tumulus"—the warrior buried centuries ago on the Downs where the young philosopher used to sit and meditate, until his mind "felt back" through the centuries and the dead were as real to him as the living.

That his self-imposed solitude aggravated the misfortunes of his later years can hardly be doubted; yet here too we feel that he was but obeying an inevitable instinct, for he could not have written the works he

---

[1] *The Dewy Morn*, i. 83.

was most desirous to write had he lived as other men live in society.[1] In no matter was his proud independence more strikingly exemplified than in his indignant refusal to make application to the "Royal Literary Fund" at a time when his poverty was the sorest; the Royal Literary Fund was to him an institution which humiliates the recipient past all bounds— he preferred to work on in drudgery and despair. Yet how fiercely he resented the thraldom of necessitous authorship may be judged from his own assertion, that he "would infinitely rather be a tallow-chandler with a good steady income and no thought than an author."

During these last years, when all else seemed failing him, his thoughts reverted more and more to the early memories of Coate, the scenes which he had held in his mind, and reproduced in his writings, with such unalterable affection. Nothing is more characteristic and pathetic than his last essay, entitled "My Old Village," in which he reviews, with the consciousness that he is a dying man, the haunts and fancies of his boyhood. "I planted myself everywhere," he says, "under the trees, in the fields and footpaths, by day and by night, and that is why I have never put myself into the charge of the many-wheeled creatures that move on the rails and gone back thither, lest I might find the trees look small, and the elms mere switches, and the fields shrunken, and the brooks dry, and no

---

[1] Mr. Frederick Greenwood expresses the opinion that Jefferies deliberately shunned society to avoid losing his "native sensibility."

voice anywhere—nothing but my own ghost to meet me by every hedge."

The last few months of his life, during which he was in a state of bodily and mental prostration, were spent at "Sea View," Goring, a square-shaped, red-tiled house, from which the shore is reached by a sunken lane which ends abruptly on the shingle. The country all around is plain, dreary, and Dutch-like, yet not without a quaint charm of its own—a flat tract lying between sea and Downs, with windmills and low spires, and fields intersected by small dykes which the sea fills at the flood. There could scarcely be a greater contrast to the scenery of Coate.

Here Jefferies died in his thirty-ninth year, on August 14th, 1887, and was buried in the neighbouring cemetery of Broadwater, on the outskirts of Worthing. "Could I have my own way after death," he had written in his *Story*, " I would be burned on a pyre of pine-wood, open to the air, and placed on the summit of the hills. Then let my ashes be scattered abroad—not collected in an urn—freely sown wide and broadcast."

This wish, like so many of his wishes, could not be gratified; but it is at least a satisfaction to know that he is buried in a singularly beautiful spot. Go there on a clear afternoon of May, when the great sun is "burning in the heaven," and the wind (the wind that whispered its secrets to Bevis!) is blowing softly through the grass, and you will find the whole cemetery ringing with the song of birds, thrushes loud on the neighbouring trees, wood-pigeons and rooks flying swiftly overhead, swallows passing and repassing, butterflies and humble-bees flitting to and fro, exactly that hum of awakening life which Jefferies so incomparably described. And here, among the birds and bees and flowers, within sight of the Downs, within hearing of the sea, lies that passionate heart whose self-told *Story* shall be read and re-read, centuries hence, with tears of pity and admiration.

II.—AS NATURALIST.

In one of his unpublished fragmentary manuscripts,[1] Richard Jefferies refers to himself as "a student of nature and human life"—not of wild nature only, be it observed, but "of nature and human life." It would be difficult to frame a briefer and more accurate description of him; yet the importance of the phrase, though wholly borne out by his writings, appears to have escaped the large majority of his literary critics, who still persist in regarding him as a "naturalist" pure and simple, an observer whose legitimate function it is to study, let us say, the migratory habits of the cuckoo, or the architectural skilfulness of the long-tailed tit, but by no means to devote attention to any of the weightier subjects of human interest and concern. Now, as a matter of fact, Jefferies was not a scientific naturalist at all, if we use the term *scientific* in its limited technical meaning. He was, as all really sympathetic readers know, a naturalist in a wider sense, a student of the natural in all its forms and phases, from the nature that is called inanimate to the nature that is called human; nay more, he was, as we shall see in a later chapter, an enthusiastic advocate of the "return

---
[1] Epitomised in *Pall Mall Gazette*, Nov. 10, 1871.

to nature," a doctrine which the scientist is apt to regard with a very unfavourable eye.

How distinctly Jefferies claimed for himself the fuller function of the naturalist may be judged from a passage in one of his letters to his publisher, written in 1882. "I want," he says, "to express the deeper feelings with which observation of life-histories has filled me, and I assure you I have as large a collection of these facts and incidents—the natural history of the heart—as I have ever written about birds and trees."

It is only necessary to look at a list of his writings to realise the absurdity of the idea that his sole business was with the fauna and flora of his native district. In his earliest essays, as we have seen, he did not treat of these matters at all, but of the various aspects and conditions of agricultural life; and even when he had turned to Nature for his theme, he wisely dealt with the subject in its entirety, assigning to man a part in the picture no less than to the wild inhabitants of forest and field.

In *Hodge and his Masters,* for example, we have a series of typical character-sketches of rustic society—the farmer, the gentleman farmer, the bailiff, the squire, the parson, the curate, the banker, the lawyer, and all the rest of the worshipful company who look to Hodge for service and support; while *Green Ferne Farm,* albeit worthless as a novel, contains many valuable pictures of hay-making, nutting, gleaning, merry-making, and various country scenes.

It is therefore a sad mistake on the part of certain critics to blame Jefferies for this perfectly reasonable and indeed necessary extension of his scope, on the ground that he "would have done well to leave Hodge and Hodge's masters alone, and keep to his beasts, and birds, and fishes."[1] His own wiser instinct prompted him to interpret the naturalist's duty in a larger sense, and to paint the country as a whole, in which Hodge and his masters and the beasts and the fishes had alike to play their part. In this same connection he remarks of Gilbert White, to a reprint of whose famous work he himself contributed a preface, that "it must ever be regretted that he did not leave a natural history of the people of his day. We should then have had a picture of England just before the beginning of our present era, and a wonderful difference it would have shown." Future naturalists will not be able to lay any such omission to Jefferies' charge, for in these books of his, as his biographer has truly observed, "the whole of the country life of the nineteenth century will be found displayed down to every detail."

"Jefferies-land" is the title which Mr. Besant appropriately bestows on the district round Coate. There are certain places which seem to be inseparably associated with the names of certain individuals; and though land reformers do wisely teach us that the soil should be held by the community, yet there are some landlords whose title-deeds will never be called in question, and some owners who will never be dispossessed of their estate. It is safe to prophesy that

---

[1] *Athenæum.*

"Jefferies-land" will afford an instance of this security of tenure, and, like White's "Selborne," will remain the inalienable property of the great nature student who made it his own. It is probable, too, that no district could have been better suited for the naturalist's purpose than this piece of typical English scenery, with its combination of rich, low-lying cornland and high grassy Downs, every feature of which is so carefully studied and transcribed in a certain phase of Jefferies' work.

I quote from the preface to *Wild Life in a Southern County*.

"Commencing at the highest spot, an ancient entrenchment on the Downs has been chosen as the starting-place from whence to explore the uplands. Beneath the hill a spring breaks forth, and tracing its course downwards there next come the village and the hamlet. Still farther the streamlet becomes a broad brook, flowing through meadows in the midst of which stands a solitary farm-house. The house itself, the garden and orchard, are visited by various birds and animals. In the fields immediately around—in the great hedges and the copse—are numerous others, and an expedition is made to the forest. Returning to the farm again as a centre, the rookery remains to be examined, and the ways and habits of the inhabitants of the hedges. Finally come the fish and wild fowl of the brook and lake;—finishing in the Vale."

It has already been stated that one of Jefferies' early instructors in the mysteries of woodcraft was a friendly gamekeeper. "What he learned of true sport," says Mr. Graham,[1] "appears to have come mainly from a neighbouring gamekeeper, his friendship for whom accounts for more than one thing in his story. It is a common practice for lads in his station of life, whether they are born sportsmen or not, to cultivate the acquaintance of the keeper. Of all rural occupations his is the most interesting, and every walk with him must have been to Jefferies a lesson in natural history. We can imagine the two walking along the headlands, or lounging through the wood, now halting to drop a jay or a magpie from its nest in the thicket, or noting to what new earth the vixen had transported her family, or resting quietly in broomy corners or sunny dyke-backs, while wild things, unwitting and fearless, crept forth from their holes."

To do Jefferies justice, he seems to have utilised these early experiences in the most business-like manner, for not only did he absorb and assimilate the esoteric instructions of the keeper, but he shrewdly proceeded to examine the converse side of the game question by doing some profitable poaching for himself, and thereby turning his mentor's precepts to good account. This is euphemistically referred to by the writer quoted above. "The part acted by sport in his life was that in these early days it supplied him with a new inducement to be abroad, and stimulated him to a closer study of wild life. It also prevented him from feeling so keenly as he might otherwise have

---

[1] *Nature in Books,* chapter on Richard Jefferies.

done the deep vexations of juvenile penury." In this way, Jefferies personally qualified himself to be the author not only of *The Gamekeeper at Home*, but also of that other correlative and complementary study, *The Amateur Poacher*.

It is undeniable that, as things now are, a taste for sport is in many cases the precursor of a taste for natural history; it is the first and lowest rung of the ladder, up which a man may gradually climb from an insensate love of death-dealing to an exalted reverence for life. It by no means follows that sport itself is commendable on this account, for it is but one man in a thousand who at present emancipates himself in this way, and the ordinary sportsman-naturalist is a very dismal person indeed; moreover, in a really enlightened state of society there would be other and better introductions to a familiarity with the open air. But taking facts as we find them, we must admit that Jefferies, like his fellow-naturalist Thoreau, owed much of his early acquaintance with nature to the practice of sport.

Now in Thoreau's case, as every reader of *Walden* knows, the killing-mania soon died away, and did not affect either his character or his writings very noticeably. He gave up shooting, and sold his gun, having come to the conclusion that "there is a finer way of studying ornithology than this," and that "no humane being, past the thoughtless age of boyhood, will wantonly murder any creature which holds its life by the same tenure that he does." But Jefferies' emergence was a slower and less complete one, and his early books are disfigured by many revolting details of the seamy side of sportsmanship, which are intolerable to any reader in whom either the humane or artistic instinct is well developed. Here is a single specimen from the chapter on "Ferreting," in *The Amateur Poacher*.

"It was always a sight to see Little John's keen delight in 'wristing' their necks. He affected utter unconsciousness of what he was doing, looked you in the face, and spoke about some indifferent subject. But all the while he was feeling the rabbit's muscles stretch before the terrible grasp of his hands, and an expression of complacent satisfaction flitted over his features as the neck gave with a sudden looseness, and in a moment what had been a living, straining creature became limp."

This is scarcely a worthy theme for the artist. Yet *The Gamekeeper at Home* and *The Amateur Poacher* are reported to be favourite volumes in English country houses, perhaps because "the Great House" is throughout treated so respectfully by the writer, who, little foreseeing his future change of opinion as to the blessings of landlordism, extols the faithful keeper as "not only a valuable servant, but a protection to all kinds of property." Even *The Amateur Poacher* is written in great measure in the interests of the game-preserver, and gives the outside view of the Great House and its dependencies, as *The Gamekeeper* gives the inside view. Both books are alike steeped in sanguinary descriptions of murderous implements and appliances—from a man-trap to a mole-trap—a very exhibition of all the rusty horrors of the country gentleman's torture-chamber. As standard works on natural history, if they are to be so regarded, they represent the rather rudimentary phase of the sportsman-scientist, who may, or may not, develop into something better. "Gentlemen interested in natural history," says Jefferies, "often commission the keeper to get them specimens of rare birds." To pay a servant to convert a beautiful living thing into a stuffed "specimen"—such is the gentlemanly way of showing an interest in nature!

Mr. P. Anderson Graham, in his interesting essay on Jefferies, has some remarks with reference to this subject of sport, and talks rather contemptuously of "false pity" and "fadmongers." Jefferies shot a rabbit, he tells us, "with as clear a conscience as that of a kestrel hawking a mouse." No doubt he did so *at first*—that is, until he began to think about it; but then, as Mr. Graham has himself noticed, he partly outgrew this childish love of killing, and substituted for it "the more refined pleasure of watching and noting." We learn, indeed, from the same authority, that Jefferies was never "a very keen or accomplished sportsman." "His writing on sport is that of a vigilant observer, not of an enthusiastic maker of big bags." Let us be thankful for this fact; but further let us note that if Jefferies (unlike the kestrel) was from the first destined to discard such predatory habits, it is at least a fair matter for regret that he did not do so at a somewhat earlier period of his literary career. We should then have been spared the intrusion of such unsightly passages as those to which I have referred.

Jefferies himself has given a candid account of the nature and extent of the partial change of feeling experienced by him.

"That watching so often stayed the shot that at last it grew to be a habit, the mere simple pleasure of seeing birds and animals, when they were quite unconscious that they were observed, being too great to be spoiled by the discharge. After carefully getting a wire over a jack; after waiting in a tree till a hare came along; after sitting in a mound till the partridges began to run together to roost; in the end the wire or gun remained unused. The same feeling has equally checked my hand in legitimate shooting: time after time I have flushed partridges without firing, and have let the hare bound over the furrow free. I have entered many woods just for the pleasure of creeping through the brake and the thickets. Destruction in itself was not the motive; it was an overpowering instinct for woods and fields. Yet woods and fields lose half their interest without a gun. I like the power to shoot, even though I may not use it." [1]

It need hardly be said that Jefferies, in so far as he indulged in sport at all, was one of the better class of sportsmen. He strongly disliked the continued multiplication of slaughter, and the unfair advantage, as he considered it, which modern sportsmen derive from the improved inventions in guns. He repeatedly deprecates the wanton killing of rare species on the banks of the Thames and elsewhere by the collector or holiday-maker. "I think," he says, "that there is

---

[1] *The Amateur Poacher.*

not a single creature, from the sand-martin and the black-headed bunting to the broad-winged heron, from the water-vole to the otter, from the minnow on one side of the tidal boundary to the porpoise on the other—big and little, beasts and birds (of prey or not)—that should not be encouraged and protected on this beautiful river, morally the property of the greatest city in the world."[1] And elsewhere, " The people of London should look upon the inhabitants of the river as peculiarly their own. Some day, perhaps, they will take possession of the fauna and flora within a certain compass of their city."

Moreover, Jefferies was no adherent of that scientific or pseudo-scientific school, which denies a reasoning power to animals. "I have observed," he says, "that almost all those whose labour lies in the field, and who go down to their business in the green meadows, admit the animal world to a share in the faculty of reason. It is the cabinet thinkers who construct a universe of automatons." This being his opinion we can readily believe that though by force of heredity and habit he was to some extent a sportsman, it was to the long hours of quiet watchfulness, far more than to any use of the gun, that he owed his great knowledge as a naturalist. Here is his own testimony :—

"This is the secret of observation: stillness, silence, and apparent indifference. In some instinctive way these wild creatures learn to distinguish when one is

---

[1] "The Modern Thames," in *The Open Air*.

or is not intent upon them in a spirit of enmity; and if very near, it is always the eye they watch. So long as you observe them, as it were, from the corner of the eyeball, sideways, or look over their heads at something beyond, it is well. Turn your glance full upon them to get a better view, and they are gone."

Numberless instances of the exercise of this faculty might be cited from Jefferies' books. He conceals himself in the long grass and bushes to watch the blackbird take its bath; he waits motionless for hours to mark the haunts and habits of the kingfisher; and even as he lies in bed in the early summer mornings, in his study-bedroom that overlooks the orchard at Coate, he is busily observing the robins, wrens, and other small birds that have plucked up sufficient courage to enter through the open window. Few of his short essays are more charming than the two entitled " A Brook " and a " London Trout,"[1] in which he tells how, during four seasons at Surbiton, he kept friendly watch over a certain goodly fish which lived under the shadow of a bridge much frequented by anglers. "There were ways and means by which he could be withdrawn without any noise or publicity. But, then, what would be the pleasure of securing him, the fleeting pleasure of an hour, compared to the delight of seeing him almost day by day? I watched him for many weeks, taking great precautions that no one should observe how continually I looked over into the water there."

---

[1] In *Nature near London*.

Jefferies had keen eyesight; but that alone would not be sufficient to account for his success as a naturalist. "There is a trick in finding birds' nests," he says, "and a trick in seeing birds. So soon as I had seen one, I saw plenty." This trick of the observer is nothing else than intense interest in his pursuit; for as another great naturalist has remarked, " You must have the bird in your heart before you can find it in the bush. The eye must have purpose and aim."[1] For the rest of it, there is much wisdom in Jefferies' precept, which was also his practice, of *beginning near home.* " Be very careful not to go too far; keep round the skirts of home, near the garden, or in the nearest field, else you will jump over the very best; for it is a fact that the greatest variety of information is generally gathered in a very small compass." Jefferies' *Nature near London* gives irrefutable proof that this principle is a sound one.

This leads us to a point much insisted on by Jefferies, that the vigilant observer has no need to go across sea for his education, since all foreign phenomena have their counterparts on English soil.

"I found, while I was shooting every day, that the reeds, and ferns, and various growths through which I pushed my way, explained to me the jungles of India, the swamps of Central Africa, and the backwoods of America; all the vegetation of the world. Representatives exist in our own woods, hedges, and fields, or by the shore of inland waters. It was the same with flowers. I think I am scientifically accurate in saying

---

[1] John Burroughs: Essay on "Sharp Eyes."

that every known plant has a relative of the same species or genus, growing wild in this country. . . . It has long been one of my fancies that this country is an epitome of the natural world, and that if anyone has come really into contact with its productions, and is familiar with them, and what they mean and represent, then he has a knowledge of all that exists on the earth."[1]

This, at first hearing, sounds fanciful enough; yet it is a fact that both Thoreau and Burrough, as keen observers as Jefferies himself, make very similar but independent assertions concerning their own localities. Emerson, in his biographical notice of Thoreau, has given details of his "whimsical" habit of extolling his native village of Concord as "the most favoured centre for natural observation," since it contained in a small compass all the phenomena that could be noted elsewhere. "I sit here," says Burroughs, "amid the junipers of the Hudson, with purpose every year to go to Florida, or the West Indies, or to the Pacific Coast, yet the seasons pass and I am still loitering, with a half-defined suspicion, perhaps, that if I remain quiet and keep a sharp look-out, these countries will come to me."

The moral to be drawn from these concurrent testimonies is that in natural history, as in other pursuits, the zeal and ability of the student are of far more importance than the place. The born naturalist always keeps in touch with nature, even when he is compelled to live near the town, a fact which can be read as

---

[1] Essay on "Sport and Science," in *The Life of the Fields*.

clearly in Burrough's essay on "Spring at the Capital" as in Jefferies' *Nature near London*. Washington or the Hudson, Surbiton or Coate—it is all one to the man who has the feeling heart and the seeing eye for Nature.

"It is usually supposed," says Jefferies, "to be necessary to go far into the country to find wild birds and animals in sufficient numbers to be pleasantly studied. Such was certainly my own impression till circumstances led me, for the convenience of access to London, to reside for awhile about twelve miles from town. There my preconceived views on the subject were quite overthrown by the presence of as much bird-life as I had been accustomed to in distant fields and woods."[1] Several of Jefferies' essays similarly treat of Nature near Brighton.

Many interesting points of comparison might be drawn out between the works of those three great nature-lovers, Thoreau, Burroughs, and Jefferies, in all of whom there is the same intense watchfulness, the same patient self-possession, the same determined concentration of eye and ear on some particular locality. It is much to be regretted, and very surprising also, considering the nature of his studies, that Jefferies had apparently no acquaintance with the writings of either of his two American fellow-naturalists. Even White's *Selborne*, for which he wrote an Introduction in 1887, was not known to him until the closing years of his life. "I did not come across Mr.

---

[1] Preface to *Nature near London*.

White's book," he says, "till late in the day, when it was in fact too late, else this calendar [White's Naturalists' Calendar'] would have been of the utmost advantage to me." And if this is true of Gilbert White's relation to Jefferies, what shall be said of Thoreau's? To have come across a copy of *Walden*, or the extracts from Thoreau's *Journal*, would have been little less than a revelation to him.[1]

In the period of Jefferies' mature work, which dates from the commencement of his residence at Surbiton, in 1877, to his death ten years later, two distinct phases are readily observable. He appears at first in the character under which we are now considering him—the naturalist who by a long and loving apprenticeship has become absolutely familiar with all the phenomena and details of country life, and can reproduce them in language of much clearness and flexibility. Nor is it any romantic and fanciful Arcadia that is depicted in his pages; for though an idealist at heart, he is also, in his descriptive writings, one of the sternest and most uncompromising of realists, and gives us the dark no less than the bright features of his story with unremitting fidelity. This is what he says in reference to the application of machinery to agriculture:

"If I were a painter I should like to paint all this. For I think that the immense realism of the iron

---

[1] It is, however, worth noting that *The Story of my Heart* was compared with Thoreau's *Walden* in an article in the *Academy* (Nov. 3, 1883) which Jefferies probably read.

wheels makes the violet yet more lovely; the more they try to drive out Nature with a fork, the more she returns, and the soul clings the stronger to the wild flowers. He who has got the sense of beauty in his eye can find it in things as they really are, and needs no stagey time of artificial pastorals to furnish him with a sham nature. Idealise to the full, but idealise the real, else the picture is a sham." [1]

These words, though written in one of Jefferies' later essays, are also applicable to the best efforts of his earlier style, which is as remarkable for its close fidelity to nature as for its idyllic beauty of expression.

The volumes which furnish the most notable instances of this earlier phase of Jefferies' genius are perhaps the four by which he is at present very generally known—*The Gamekeeper at Home, The Amateur Poacher, Wild Life in a Southern County*, and *Round about a Great Estate*, in all of which he manifests the same extraordinary knowledge of the fauna and flora of his native district, a knowledge based on an exceptionally keen habit of observation, and strengthened by a powerful memory and a diligent course of journal-keeping. To these, as before stated, must be added *Hodge and his Masters*, where the human animal is subjected to the same careful study, and *Green Ferne Farm*, in which Jefferies attempted to combine the qualities of novelist and naturalist.

---

[1] "Walks in the Wheatfields," in *Field and Hedgerow*.

That a permanent historical value will attach to writings of this kind can hardly be doubted; they will be studied years hence, along with White's *Selborne* and a few similar works, as a chronicle of natural history—a museum to which artists and scientists will repair for instruction and entertainment. I cannot, however, at all agree with those of Jefferies' admirers who consider these volumes (to wit, the *Gamekeeper at Home*, and the rest of the same class) to be his literary masterpieces, and who speak of them as exhibiting, in contrast with his later books, what they call his "simpler and better style." I believe, with Mr. Walter Besant, that Jefferies' word-pictures of the country life are "far from being the most considerable part of his work." Certain advantages there are, beyond question, in the simple treatment of a clear, well-defined subject, the importance of which, so far as it goes, is universally recognised, and is not complicated by any admixture of religious mysticism or social controversy; such writing is at once more popular and less perilous than that which Jefferies afterwards went on to attempt. But a man's best and highest work is not necessarily that which is most successfully undertaken or most widely appreciated; nor is there anything at all conclusive in the fact that Jefferies' earlier volumes have a hundred readers where his later have ten. In the present state of "humane letters" such a verdict was inevitable, but it is none the less a verdict that will some day be rescinded.

I therefore regard this period of Jefferies' authorship, during which he worked and wrote as a "naturalist" (in the sense of a student and observer of the country life, and no more than the country life) as simply a necessary step in his progression to greater achievements. It marks an immense advance on his own juvenile productions, but it is itself almost equally inferior to the work that was to follow. It exhibits a vast knowledge of the subjects of which he treats, and more than enough real literary merit to give it distinction and popularity among a not too discriminating public. It is well, then, that Jefferies should be appreciated in this capacity, but it must not be forgotten that he does not end here; the mere fact that he felt impelled to go on to other and more complex work is a sufficient indication that he was born to be something more than a naturalist. It would be laughable that in booksellers' catalogues, and even on the title-pages of his own volumes, he is so commonly designated—apparently on the assumption that this is his literary masterpiece—as "author of *The Gamekeeper at Home*," were it not that a useful purpose is perhaps served in reminding us of an identity which it might otherwise be hard to remember. That the hand which wrote *The Scarlet Shawl* in 1874 should have written *The Gamekeeper at Home* in 1878 is wonderful indeed, but it is not less wonderful that the author of *The Gamekeeper at Home* should have developed within five years into the author of *The Story of my Heart*. None of the recorded curiosities of natural history can beat that.

III.—AS POET-NATURALIST.

There has arisen during the last half-century a certain class of literature, of which the chief exponents have been aptly designated "poet-naturalists."[1] Since the time when old Gilbert White devoted himself, in his homely and prosaic fashion, to the duty of observing and chronicling the fauna and flora of his Hampshire village, the literary treatment of natural history has been expanded and exalted no less than the poetical conception of Nature itself; with the result that the idealistic tendency of modern poetry, taking form in an intense sympathy with woods and fields and streams, has affected and permeated even such apparently matter-of-fact studies as zoology and botany. Still more has the naturalist of the human—the "student of nature and human life," as Jefferies expressed it—been influenced by this movement, which tends to combine the power of minute and patient investigation with the exercise of a more imaginative faculty than the anthropologist has hitherto possessed.

Now, of course, in Jefferies' case it is impossible to draw any hard-and-fast line, or to indicate the precise

---

[1] The name was applied to Thoreau by his friend and biographer, Ellery Channing.

point at which the naturalist ends and the poet-naturalist begins. There are many unmistakable traces of the latter character in his earlier books, as, for example, in the following passage of *Wild Life*:

"The joy in life of these animals—indeed, of almost all animals and birds in freedom—is very great. You may see it in every motion: in the lissom bound of the hare, the playful leap of the rabbit, the song that the lark and the finch *must* sing; the soft, loving coo of the dove in the hawthorn; the blackbird ruffling out his feathers on a rail. The sense of living—the consciousness of seeing and feeling—is manifestly intense in them all, and is in itself an exquisite pleasure. . . . . On outspread wings the swallow floats above, then slants downwards with a rapid swoop, and with the impetus of the motion rises easily. Therefore it is that this skull here, lying so light in the palm of the hand, with the bright sunshine falling on it, and a shadowy darkness in the vacant orbits of the eyes, fills us with sadness. 'As leaves on leaves, so men on men decay;' how much more so with these creatures whose generations are so short."

But though there is no lack of such isolated poetical sentiments in Jefferies' earlier works, by which I mean the works published between 1878 and 1881, it is no exaggeration to say that the latter date marks the commencement of an essentially new style; for whereas the poet in Jefferies had hitherto been accessory and subordinate to the naturalist, the position is now reversed, and we find the poetical and imaginative element wielding almost complete supremacy over the merely descriptive and scientific.[1] "He took the step," says his biographer, "the vast step, across the chasm which separates the poetic from the vulgar mind, and began to clothe the real with the colours and glamour of the unreal; to write down the response of the soul to the phenomena of Nature; to interpret the voice of Nature speaking to the soul."

Another admirer of Jefferies has drawn a suggestive distinction between that portion of his writings "which is made up of *observation*, and that which breathes *aspiration*."[2]

In this aspect of Jefferies we are reminded of George Meredith's "Melampus":—

" Divinely thrilled was the man, exultingly full,
   As quick well-waters that come of the heart of earth,
  Ere yet they dart in a brook are one bubble-pool
   To light and sound, wedding both at the leap of birth.
The soul of light vivid shone, a stream within stream;
  The soul of sound from a musical shell outflew;
Where others hear but a hum and see but a beam,
  The tongue and eye of the fountain of life he knew."

The volumes which mark this most important transition are *Wood Magic* and *Bevis*, published in 1881 and 1882 respectively, in both of which the central idea is the intimate sympathetic converse that

---

[1] *Red Deer*, 1884, is in some respects a return to the earlier style.

[2] Edward Garnett, article on Richard Jefferies, *Universal Review*, 1888.

exists, or is imagined to exist, between childhood and Nature.[1]

The character of Bevis, the boy-hero of both stories, in spite of the tedious length of the narrative, is one of the most charming of Jefferies' creations, and has far more vitality than most of the figures in his novels. For Bevis, apart from his adventurous wanderings and voyages (which interest us chiefly as being actual records of Jefferies' own boyish freaks and imaginings), is the special favourite and confidant of Nature and her familiars—it is to him that the wild animals and birds, the trees and flowers, the streams and winds and sunshine, reveal their pass-words and secrets. The well-known passages that describe Bevis' communings with the Wind are not only the best thing in *Wood Magic*, but the most significant indication of Jefferies' new departure, for both in depth of feeling and power of expression they entirely transcend anything previously written by him. Says the Wind:—

"Bevis, my love, if you want to know all about the sun, and the stars, and everything, make haste and come to me, and I will tell you, dear. In the morning, dear, get up as quick as you can, and drink me as I come down from the hill. In the day go up on the hill, dear, and drink me again, and stay there if you can till the stars shine out, and drink still more of me.

"And by and by you will understand all about the sun, and the moon, and the stars, and the Earth which is so beautiful, Bevis. It is so beautiful, you can

---

[1] See also "Saint Guido," in *The Open Air*. The child Guido seems to be Bevis under another name.

hardly believe how beautiful it is. Do not listen, dear, not for one moment, to the stuff and rubbish they tell you down there in the houses where they will not let me come. If they say the Earth is not beautiful, tell them they do not speak the truth. But it is not their fault, for they have never seen it, and as they have never drank me their eyes are closed, and their ears shut up tight. But every evening, dear, before you get into bed, do you go to your window, and lift the curtain and look up at the sky, and I shall be somewhere about, or else I shall be quiet in order that there may be no clouds, so that you may see the stars. In the morning, as I said before, rush out and drink me up."

In the later volumes, of which *Wood Magic* was the precursor, this mystic nature-worship is everywhere dominant. It is no longer child-life only that is credited with the wondrous secret; for Jefferies now writes without disguise as one who has received a solemn revelation of the inner beauty of the universe —the wind, the sea, the sunlight, the leaves, the mere dull earth-clods, all are alike sacred to him. "Never was such a worshipper of earth," he exclaims of himself. "The commonest pebble, dusty and marked with the stain of the ground, seems to me so wonderful; my mind works round it till it becomes the sun and centre of a system of thought and feeling. Sometimes moving aside the tufts of grass with careless fingers while resting on the sward, I found these little pebble-stones loose in the crumbly earth among the rootlets. Then, brought out from the shadow, the sunlight shone and glistened on the particles of sand that adhered to it.

Particles adhered to my skin—thousands of years between finger and thumb, these atoms of quartz, and sunlight shining all that time, and flowers blooming and life glowing in all, myriads of living things, from the cold still limpet on the rock to the burning throbbing heart of man."

Or take that marvellous account in *The Story of My Heart* of his sudden brief pilgrimage to the sea:—

"There was a time when a weary restlessness came upon me, perhaps from too-long-continued labour. It was like a drought—a moral drought—as if I had been absent for many years from the sources of life and hope. The inner nature was faint, all was dry and tasteless; I was weary for the pure fresh springs of thought. Some instinctive feeling uncontrollable drove me to the sea. . . . I found the sea at last; I walked beside it in a trance away from the houses out into the wheat. The ripe corn stood up to the beach, the waves on one side of the shingle, and the yellow wheat on the other.

"There, alone, I went down to the sea. I stood where the foam came to my feet, and looked out over the sunlit waters. The great earth bearing the richness of the harvest, and its hills golden with corn, was at my back; its strength and firmness under me. The great sun shone above, the wide sea was before me, the wind came sweet and strong from the waves. The life of the earth and the sea, the glow of the sun filled me; I touched the surge with my hand, I lifted my face to the sun, I opened my lips to the wind. I prayed aloud in the roar of the waves—my soul was strong as the sea, and prayed with the sea's might. Give me fulness of life like to the sea and the sun, and to the earth and the air; give me fulness of physical life, mind equal and beyond their fulness; give me a greatness and perfection of soul higher than all things; give me my inexpressible desire which swells in me like a tide—give it to me with all the force of the sea."

We thus perceive that what had at first been ostensibly little more than an instinctive love of wild scenery and free out-door pursuits, and a powerful capacity for noting and commemorating the various features of country life, was gradually transformed and expanded into a deliberate personal faith, as Jefferies began more clearly to apprehend the meaning of that "ideal of nature," which, for him, embraced and affected human aspirations and human art no less than the nature which is (or is supposed to be) non-human and inanimate. It is in one of his latest essays, "Nature in the Louvre,"[1] that we find the clearest expression of this creed. Pondering long by the statue of the "Stooping Venus," he thus connects the ideal beauty of Nature with the ideal good of man:—

"Old days which I had spent wandering among the deep meadows and by green woods came back to me. In such days the fancy had often occurred to me that besides the loveliness of leaves and flowers, there must be some secret influence drawing me on as a hand might beckon. The light and colour suspended in the summer atmosphere, as colour is in stained but translucent glass, were to me always on the point of becoming tangible in some beautiful form. The hovering lines and shape never became sufficiently defined for me to know what form it could be, yet

---

[1] In *Field and Hedgerow*.

the colours and the light meant something which I was not able to fix. I was now sitting in a gallery of stone, with cold marbles, cold floors, cold light from the windows. Without, there were only houses, the city of Paris—a city above all other cities farthest from woods and meads. Here, nevertheless, there came back to me this old thought born in the midst of flowers and wind-rustled leaves, and I saw that with it the statue before me was in concord. The living original of this work was the human impersonation of the secret influence which had beckoned me on in the forest and by running streams. She expressed in loveliness of form the colour and light of sunny days; she expressed the deep aspiring desire of the soul for the perfection of the frame in which it is encased, for the perfection of its own existence. . . . Though I cannot name the ideal good, it seems to me that it will be in some way closely associated with the ideal beauty of nature."

It has already been hinted that Jefferies' London experiences, which first awakened his mind to a more vivid interest in those great human problems which a crowded civilisation must needs face, form a sort of link between his position as a naturalist and his position as a thinker. "Nature," he says in his *Story*, "was deepened by the crowds and foot-worn stones." In certain moods he delighted in London; partly, perhaps, for the mere sensuous pleasure of the rich spectacles to be seen there (he says in *Amaryllis* that "to anyone with an eye the best entertainment in the world is a lounge in London streets"), partly also because he could there stimulate his faculty for philosophic meditation. "I am quite as familiar with

London as with the country," he wrote to a correspondent. "Some people have the idea that my knowledge is confined to the fields; as a matter of fact, I have had quite as much to do with London—all parts of it, too—and am very fond of what I may call a thickness of the people such as exists there. I like the solitude of the hills, and the hum of the most crowded city; I dislike little towns and villages. I dream in London quite as much as in the woodlands. It's a wonderful place to dream in."[1]

The obvious exaggeration in Jefferies' statement that he was "quite as familiar" with London as with the country, must be set down to the irritating effect of the common but fallacious assumption that the ardent nature lover is unable to appreciate the impressive features of the town. It is quite true that Jefferies, like Thoreau and other poet-naturalists who might be named, could not exist for any lengthy period away from the life of the fields; true also that he remarked, in very uncomplimentary terms, on some of the hideous deformities which a crowded society begets. In his essay on "The London Road," for example, he has a pitiless physiognomical criticism of "the London leer."

"That hideous leer is so repulsive—one cannot endure it—but it is so common; you see it on the

---

[1] Compare Thoreau's letter to Emerson from New York, May 23, 1843. "There are two things I hear, and am aware I live in the neighbourhood of—the roar of the sea and the hum of the city."

faces of four-fifths of the ceaseless stream that runs out from the ends of the earth of London into the green sea of the country. It disfigures the faces of the carters who go with the waggons and other vehicles; it defaces—absolutely defaces—the workmen who go forth with vans, with timber, with carpenters' work, and the policeman standing at the corners, in London itself particularly. The London leer hangs on their faces."[1]

Again, in his *After London*—the very title of which is opprobrious to the patriotic citizen—he draws a sombre picture of the ruins of a defunct civilisation, the pestilent fen which is the sole remnant and residue of the former metropolis of the world. Not even that "City of Dreadful Night" of the pessimist-poet's imagination is more lurid than the scene of which Jefferies' hero is the witness, when he "had penetrated into the midst of that dreadful place, of which he had heard many a tradition; how the earth was poison, the water poison, the air poison, the very light of heaven, falling through such an atmosphere, poison."[2]

But in spite of such passages, Jefferies was keenly sensitive—as sensitive almost as De Quincey himself — to the charm of the great city, and has established a good claim to be reckoned among the foremost of London's eulogists. Like De Quincey, he has pictured the feeling of unrest and irresistible attraction

---

[1] "On the London Road," in *The Open Air*.

[2] Contrast with this the optimistic description of a ruralised and humanised London, in William Morris's *News from Nowhere*.

that London exercises on all the surrounding districts. "There is a fascination in it; there is a magnetism stronger than that of the rock which drew the nails from Sindbad's ship. It is not business, for you may have none in the ordinary sense, it is not "society," it is not pleasure. It is the presence of man in his myriads. There is something in the heart which cannot be satisfied away from it." He even claims a world-wide scope for this radiating influence. "London," he thinks, "is the only *real* place in the world. The cities turn towards London as young partridges run to their mother. The cities know that they are not real. They are only houses, and wharves, and bridges, and stucco; only outside. The minds of all men in them, merchants, artists, thinkers, are bent on London. San Francisco thinks London; so does St. Petersburg."

Some of the very best of Jefferies' short essays are devoted to London scenes; for example, those on "Sunlight in a London Square," "Venice in the East End," and "The Pigeons at the British Museum," all of which are included, rather oddly, perhaps, in the volume entitled, *The Life of the Fields,* where, as if to account for this apparent incongruity, the author remarks in a foot-note that "the sunlight and the wind enter London, and the life of the fields is there too, if you will but see it." In *The Open Air*, again, we find him writing of "Red Roofs of London," and other similar themes; but it is in *The Story of My Heart* that he gives the fullest prominence to these studies of London life. No reader of that book can ever forget the wonderful descriptions of an early summer morning on London Bridge, of the visits to the pictures at the National Gallery, and the Greek statues at the Museum, and, above all, of the streams of human life in front of the Royal Exchange.

"I used to come and stand near the apex of the promontory of pavement which juts out towards the pool of life; I still go there to ponder. Burning in the sky, the sun shone on me as when I rested in the narrow valley carved in prehistoric time. Burning in the sky, I can never forget the sun. The heat of summer is dry there as if the light carried an impalpable dust; dry, breathless heat that will not let the skin respire, but swathes up the dry fire in the blood. But beyond the heat and light, I felt the presence of the sun as I felt it in the solitary valley, the presence of the resistless forces of the universe; the sun burned in the sky as I stood and pondered. Is there any theory, philosophy, or creed, is there any system or culture, any formulated method able to meet and satisfy each separate item of this agitated pool of human life? By which they may be guided, by which hope, by which look forward? Not a mere illusion of the craving heart—something real, as real as the solid walls of fact against which, like drifted seaweed, they are dashed; something to give each separate personality sunshine and a flower in its own existence now; something to shape this million-handed labour to an end and outcome that will leave more sunshine and more flowers to those who must succeed?"

We see, then, that the mysticism which is so marked a feature of Jefferies' later writings was in part a London growth, for it was not until *after* these reveries on bridge and pavement that his vision faculty found expression. The leading thought by which his autobiographical *Story* is inspired is the intense and passionate yearning for what he calls "soul-life." Not content with those three ideas which he says the primeval cavemen wrested from the unknown darkness around them—the existence of the soul, immortality, and the deity—he desires to wrest "a fourth, and still more than a fourth, from the darkness of thought." He believes that we are even now on the verge of great spiritual discoveries, that "a great life, an entire civilisation, lies just outside the pale of common thought," and that these soul-secrets may be won by a resolute and sustained endeavour of the human mind. This "fourth idea," which cannot be formulated in words, since there are no words to express it, is the conception of a possible soul-life which is above and beyond the ideas of existence and immortality, beyond even deity itself; a spiritual entity which is even now realised in part by the absorption of the soul, in rapturous moments of reverie and devotion, into the beauty and infinity of the visible universe. In this we are often reminded of De Quincey; but in Jefferies' case there was a more distinct purpose and a deliberate perseverance in the search after the unknown.

But while the "soul-life" formed the first portion of what Jefferies calls his "prayer," the physical life was by no means forgotten or undervalued. His second aspiration is for perfection of physical beauty, the human form being to him the sum and epitome of all that is impressive in nature. To cultivate bodily strength and symmetry is as real and indispensable a duty as to aspire to soul-life, since "to be shapely of form is so infinitely beyond wealth, power, fame, all that ambition can give, that these are dust before it." Seldom have the glories of physical existence—the "wild joys of living," as Browning calls them—been celebrated with such rapturous devotion as in Jefferies' prose poem. Day and night are declared by him to be too short for their full enjoyment—the day should be sixty hours long, the night should offer forty hours of sleep. "Oh, beautiful human life!" he exclaims. "Tears come in my eyes as I think of it. So beautiful, so inexpressibly beautiful!"

We speak of Jefferies as a mystic; but it must not be forgotten that his is the mysticism of no mere visionary of the study or the cloister, but of one of the keenest and most painstaking observers that ever set eyes on nature; a mysticism which, as he himself asserts, is based not on the imaginary, but the real. "From standing face to face so long with the real earth, the real sun, and the real sea, I am firmly convinced that there is an immense range of thought quite unknown to us yet." The passages in *The Story of My Heart*, where he seems to be dimly groping his way on the very confines of this spiritual dreamland, and striving to express in words ideas which he knows can only be apprehended by the emotions, are among the most moving and impressive in recent literature; none but Jefferies could have written them, so rich are they in their confident anticipation of future intellectual discoveries, so tenderly pathetic in the sadness of their personal retrospect.

On the subject of the ecstatic trance or "prayer," which is so often alluded to in Jefferies' autobiography, I will here give the concluding portion of those *Notes on Richard Jefferies* which have already been quoted.[1]

"Jefferies' 'hysteria' is the index to psychical peculiarities that aid us in comprehending one important factor which enters into the making of his unique *Story*. That book is one of the most singular products to be found in any literature. It is an incomplete history of reminiscences of experiences in an unusual bodily condition, and one which Jefferies had the power to induce at will. At first he required for its production a peculiar environment, but later in his short life he was independent of his surroundings, and could project himself into these singular conditions as readily amidst all the roaring din of a London street as when rambling by a babbling brook, or standing alone on that silent hill-top which he depicts in the first chapter of his autobiography.

"This peculiar condition is simply that *ecstasy* in which all mystics have delighted; and in Chapter V. of the *Story*, Jefferies has innocently enough described the *methodus operandi* of his 'projection,' to borrow a word from the alchemists.

"'I looked at the hills, at the dewy grass, and then up through the elm branches to the sky. In a moment all that was behind me, the house, the people, the sound, seemed to disappear, and to leave me alone. Involuntarily I drew a long breath, then I breathed slowly. My thought, or inner consciousness, went up through the illumined sky, and I was lost in a moment of exaltation. This lasted only a very short time, perhaps only a part of a second, and while it

[1] See p. 25.

lasted there was no formulated wish. I was absorbed; I drank the beauty of the morning; I was exalted.'

"Jefferies must have acquired this trick of self-projection unconsciously; he certainly was equally unaware of what he was learning, and of the psychical consequences of such learning. There is no evidence extant that he understood the physiological relationship between his drawing a long breath—deep inspiration—and then breathing slowly, and the succeeding momentary exaltation; but that process so changes the cerebral circulation that his brief absorption, 'only a part of a second,' is readily accounted for by the physiologist.

"In saying that Jefferies was not aware of what he was learning, it is implied that he had not read any East Indian literature, and thereby learned to practise the *yoga*. Of course the method employed by the Indian adept is much more complex than that followed by Jefferies, but at least one essential element for both is the peculiar respiration. As Jefferies began this occult practice while in his very teens, it is safe to conclude that it was an involuntary and unconscious discovery of his own.

"In the succeeding 'moment of exaltation,' he does not appear to have recognised any relationship of cause and effect between it and the preceding respiratory procedure, and this gives a charm to his *Story* that otherwise were wanting. His is not the baneful sensuous, De Quincey opium-deliriation; he felt a purer delight than that which inspired the visions of Kubla Khan; he saw no 'damsel with a dulcimer,' but thrilled with yearning unspeakable for the 'fuller soul,' and felt in every trembling fibre of his frame the consciousness of incarnated immortality. If this was deliriation, it was the pure breath of Nature that produced it; if, on the contrary, it was a vision of glories ineffable, it was inspired by the very winds of heaven.

"On first reading *The Story of my Heart*, I found in it a weird quality that I was wholly at a loss to account for, but while pondering upon the passage wherein he describes the method of his self-projection, the solution was at hand. His 'moments of exaltation' shadowed themselves in his *Story*, and they are reflected upon the reader according to his receptivity —the more one is *en rapport* with Jefferies, the more deeply will he be moved by these occult adumbrations.

"The recollection of those 'moments of exaltation,' remained with Jefferies after he had returned from his Pisgah to the coarser realities of common life. It was to him as if the heavens had opened, 'only a part of a second,' but that flashing glimpse had filled his heart with hunger, and his soul with yearning that not all the beauty of the earth could ever appease. Then came surging from his soul that passionate prayer for 'the fuller life,' because he, too, had come to know

> "'That boundless hunger of the immortals
> Which only God's infinitude supplies.'"

In a characteristic essay on "The Lions in Trafalgar Square,"[1] there is a reference to the above-mentioned "ecstasy," which should be compared with the earlier passage in the *Story*:

"At summer noontide, when the day surrounds us, and it is broad light even in the shadow, I like to stand by one of the lions and yield to the old feeling.

---

[1] In *The Toilers of the Field*, 1892, a posthumous collection of essays.

E

The sunshine glows on the dusky creature, as it seems, not only on the surface, but under the skin, as if it came up from out of the limb. The roar of the rolling wheels sinks and becomes distant as the sound of a waterfall when dreams are coming. All the abundant human life is smoothed and levelled, the abruptness of the individual lost in the flowing current, like separate flowers drawn along in a border, like music heard so far off that the notes are molten and the theme only remains. . . . Such a moment cannot endure long; gradually the roar deepens, the current resolves into individuals, the houses return—it is only a square."

Elsewhere in the same article, Jefferies pronounces the Trafalgar Square lions to be truer and more real than those at the Zoo; they are "lions to whom has been added the heart of a man." The naturalist will smile at this; the poet-naturalist will understand it. It is a remark which may well serve to typify the great change that came over Jefferies' whole manner of feeling and thought during his maturer and more idealistic period. In his earlier work we find abundant evidence of the watchful eye, the unfailing memory, and the artistic touch; the "heart of a man" is in his later work.

It is this humanising element in Jefferies that brings him into line with Thoreau and other writers of the poet-naturalist school. It has been said that he has much in common with George Borrow,[1] and certainly the two were so far akin as being genuine children of nature and lovers of the wild. But Bor-

---

[1] Dr. R. Garnett: article on Jefferies in *National Dictionary of Biography*.

row belongs in reality to another and different class of character—the careless, unconscious nature-lover, who is content to take his joy of sky and meadow and woodland, without asking the why or wherefore or philosophising on the fact; he was, moreover, an example of a simple reversion to a primitive type, a strange, wild growth in the cultivated garden of our modern civilisation. Jefferies, on the other hand, was eminently modern and meditative and introspective; like Thoreau, he studied and questioned and idealised Nature, and did not merely accept and assimilate her; while personally he had nothing of the adventurous spirit, dogged resolution, and quaint eccentric humour of the author of *Lavengro* and *Romany Rye*.

If Thoreau be excepted, or perhaps even without that exception, the poet-naturalist to whom Jefferies offers most striking points of resemblance (in spite of equally striking differences) is Edward Carpenter. Readers of *Towards Democracy* and *The Story of my Heart* will find in both books the same frank, sensuous joyousness, the same instinctive worship of sun and earth and sea, the same mystic adoration of the human form as the supreme embodiment of all natural beauty. To those who are inclined to follow up the question of the origin and significance of the ecstatic reveries described in Jefferies' *Story*, I would recommend a careful study of certain notable chapters in a recent work by Carpenter,[1] in which the difficult and

---

[1] *From Adam's Peak to Elephanta*, chapters viii.-xi. Swan Sonnenschein & Co.

complex subject of the Oriental practice of the *yoga* is set forth with a luminous impressiveness which contrasts strongly with the repellent jargon of many "occult" writers. It seems to be too often forgotten that all memorable experiences, whether spiritual or material, require proportionate power for their expression, and that it is possible to stultify the occult, like any other subject, by a mean and inadequate presentment of it. Of the inefficiency of all words as a vehicle of new ideas, complaint is repeatedly made in the *Story;* but it is interesting to note with what measure of success such real masters of language as Jefferies and Carpenter have surmounted this difficulty.

But, when all is said, Jefferies' position among the poet-naturalists remains a peculiar and unique one. His restless, passionate, emotional temperament differentiates him sharply from those other writers to whom he is in some measure akin—from the stern self-contented simplicity of his predecessor, Thoreau, and from the masculine energy and robustness of his contemporary, Burroughs; there is a touch of morbidness in his genius, from which Edward Carpenter's saner and more widely sympathetic idealism is entirely free. We perceive in Jefferies' personality, and in those essays by which his personality is most clearly expressed, an eager, insatiable, almost feverish craving for ideal beauty, for physical perfection, for ampler "soul-life;" he had bartered his peace in this world for a few momentary glimpses into the secrets of the world beyond. Like the "frail form" in Shelley's *Adonais,—*

"He, as I guess,
Had gazed on Nature's naked loveliness,
Actæon-like, and now he fled astray
With feeble steps o'er the world's wilderness,
And his own thoughts, along that rugged way,
Pursued, like raging hounds, their father and their prey."

IV.—AS THINKER.

SIMULTANEOUSLY with Jefferies' advance from natural history to nature-worship, a deeper and stronger feeling on social and religious subjects was manifested in his writings, and he now at last found utterance for his own distinctive judgment on many questions of great intellectual importance which had hitherto, perhaps of necessity, gone unmentioned by him. I have already referred to him as an advocate of the creed which may be summed up in the well-known phrase, "the Return to Nature"; and though certain of his critics ignore or deprecate this didactic side of his genius, and if they could have had their way, would have sent him back (like Keats to his gallipots) to the less hazardous and less disturbing topics of "his beasts and birds and fishes," I maintain on the contrary that his best and most memorable work is precisely that in which he gives free scope to these instinctive personal aspirations, the human ideal which was the true end and outcome of all his studies of wild nature.

Now, this "Return to Nature" is a theme which in one form or another, notably in the various traditions of a past Golden Age, has from time immemorial exercised a powerful attraction on the minds of poets and idealists. Considered more especially as a modern movement, it is commonly, and rightly, associated in its origin with the name of Rousseau. It was in Rousseau that the study of natural scenery and natural instinct, released at length from the thraldom of mediæval superstition, which had for centuries laid its ban on wild nature as the supposed ally and stronghold of the Evil One, found its pre-ordained champion and evangelist. It was he who first, among eighteenth-century philosophers, transformed and elevated what had hitherto been at best but a pious opinion, or a poet's fancy, into a religious creed, a deliberate ethical conviction. His strong insistence on the superiority of the country life, at a time when culture and intelligence were assumed to be inseparable from the city; his thrilling descriptions of mountains, forests, waterfalls, and the great forces of Nature, in an age when wildness was held to be almost synonymous with deformity; his rapturous praise of simplicity in education, dress, diet, manners, and the whole system of living, when society was steeped in every sort of artificiality and self-indulgence —this it was that marked the commencement of a new spirit of reverential sympathy with Nature, a passionate appeal from the conventional to the innate, which was one of the most characteristic features of the revolutionary era, and was destined to have momentous consequences for European politics and literature.

The influence of Rousseau, in the direction of greater naturalness and simplicity, showed itself in many branches of English thought. Wordsworth and the Lake school owed much to him; Godwin, Shelley, and the revolutionary writers no less; while the poet-naturalists of a later period, among whom the most prominent are Thoreau, Jefferies, and Carpenter, must be considered his lineal descendants in their treatment of all problems relating to the comparative merits of nature and civilisation. "Simplification of religion," says one of Rousseau's biographers,[1] "by clearing away the overgrowth of errors, simplification of social relations by equality, of literature and art by constant return to nature, of manners by industrious homeliness and thrift—this is the revolutionary process and ideal."

It must be understood, however, that this return to nature by no means implies a relapse into mere animalism and savagery, the question before us being not an alternative between modern "civilisation" on the one hand, and primitive barbarism on the other, but the feasibility of combining on a still higher plane the advantages incidental to either mode of life. According to the theory of one of Rousseau's most gifted successors,[2] both savagery and civilisation (in the present sense of the word) are necessary stages in human development, but we are destined hereafter to reach a third and altogether higher condition, in which, while retaining the vast intellectual advantages

---

[1] *Rousseau*, by John Morley, i. 5.
[2] See Edward Carpenter's *Civilisation, its Cause and Cure*, 1889.

of civilised society, we shall recover what we have now temporarily lost, the self-contained calmness and superb physical health of the "noble savage." Thus the future race will be both natural and civilised—civilised in its retention and enjoyment of the self-knowledge which intellectual culture can alone bestow, and natural in its still greater regard for the sacred innocence and healthfulness of unsophisticated instinct. The return to nature is an abandonment not of the benefits but of the evils of the civilised state, a reversion not to the vices but to the virtues of wild natural life.

Explicit disavowal of any retrogressive tendency has been made by all the great poet-naturalists, from Rousseau to Jefferies; nevertheless the critics still continue to misunderstand them.[1] In Jefferies' case, as in the others, this misunderstanding could scarcely have arisen had his own statements received due weight; for in his applications of the destructive nature-test to the conventionalities of modern life, there is a clear denial of any reactionary or anti-social intention.

"My sympathies and hopes are with the light of the future, only I should like it to come from Nature. The clock should be read by the sunshine, not the sun timed by the clock. The latter is indeed impossible, for though all the clocks in the world should declare

---

[1] Even in Mr. Edward Garnett's admirable and sympathetic article on Jefferies (*Universal Review*, November, 1888), we find the complaint that such men as Rousseau and Jefferies "cry that man must turn back and begin afresh; but they ask an impossibility, for man progresses."

the hour of dawn to be midnight, the sun will presently rise just the same."[1]

"All things seem possible in the open air"—in these few words we have an epitome of Jefferies' philosophy of Nature. All life, whether social or individual, that is permanently divorced from communion with the vitalising influences of free air and sunshine, will be a stunted and diseased life; and to the long disuse and degradation of natural instinct, until artificiality has become dominant in every phase of our existence, must be attributed the present numerous evils of civilised mankind. "It's indoors, sir, as kills half the people," he makes his gamekeeper say; "being indoors three parts of the day, and next to that, taking too much drink and vittals." In this simple but pregnant remark lies the germ (then undeveloped and almost unsuspected) of all his subsequent thought, the nature-creed which impelled him, in his later writings, to attack with scathing criticism the traditional in-door sophisms of education, of literature, of science, of philanthropy, of ethics, of religion—in a word, of all those respectable and time-honoured institutions of which he himself had been a supporter in his youth.

For very emphatic—emphatic to the verge of recklessness—is Jefferies' rejection of the accumulated teaching of tradition and experience. We must begin wholly afresh, and admit that the past has utterly failed, that the present is failing now; for thus alone,

---

[1] Preface to *Round about a Great Estate*.

from disbelief, can the new and saving belief be originated. "Nothing has as yet been of any value, however good its intent. There is no virtue, or reputed virtue, which has not been rigidly pursued, and things have remained as before. Everything is in vain. The circle of ideas we possess is too limited to aid us."

So, too, of modern doctrines and discoveries—they may add to the convenience, but not the real happiness of the race. The improvement of mechanism, the piling up of fortunes, the building of cities, even the teachings of science, are of no avail toward hastening the perfection of the human soul or the human body; wonderful as they are, they are for the most part valueless. The specialist finds no favour with Jefferies. "The longer people do one thing," he says, "the worse they do it, till in the end they cannot do it at all." Our whole manner of thought must be altered before true progress can become possible; men must work "not for bread, but for their souls." We must discard the present philosophy of work as a good in itself, in the knowledge that centuries of labour have but resulted in the demoralisation of the few and the degradation of the many; we must recognise that "the highest purpose of study is the education of the soul."

This education, Jefferies tells us, must be sought direct from Nature.

"All of you with little children, and who have no need to count expense, or even if you have such need, take them somehow into the country among green grass and yellow wheat, among trees, by hills and streams, if you wish their highest education, that of the heart and the soul, to be accomplished.

"Therein shall they find a Secret—a knowledge not to be written, not to be found in books. They shall know the sun and the wind, the running water, and the breast of the broad earth. Under the green spray, among the hazel boughs where the nightingale sings, they shall find a Secret, a feeling, a sense that fills the heart with an emotion never to be forgotten. They will forget the books—they will never forget the grassy fields.

"If you wish your children to think deep things, to know the holiest emotions, take them to the woods and hills, and give them the freedom of the meadows." [1]

Again and again throughout his later essays, he insists in similar mood on the hollowness of mere book-learning. Sitting in the reading-room of the British Museum, he realises "the crushing hopelessness of books, useless, not equal to one bubble borne along on the running brook I had walked by, giving no thought like the spring when I lifted the water in my hand and saw the light gleam on it." To seek the human ideal as reflected in the face of Nature—here is the true and only secret of education.

This insistence on an ideal humanity, as the visible goal by which all progress must be measured, made Jefferies dissent not only from the orthodox educational methods, but also from many of the accepted axioms and conclusions of contemporary science. He maintains, like Edward Carpenter, that science is in-

---

[1] *The Dewy Morn.*

fallible only when "it is in conjunction with the human ideal"; and he boldly refuses to acknowledge the inevitability of such scientific dogmas as the law of cause and effect, and the *it must follow* of the logician.

"However carefully the argument be built up, even though apparently flawless, there is no such thing at present as *it must follow*. . . . I think there are things exempt from mechanical rules. The restriction of thought to purely mechanical grooves blocks progress in the same way as the restrictions of mediæval superstition. Let the mind think, dream, imagine; let it have perfect freedom. To shut out the soul is to put us back more than twelve thousand years."

But if some of the most distinctive merits of Jefferies as a thinker are comprised in this essentially human aspect of his nature-creed, it is in connection with the same subject that we note his most serious defects. Admirable as is the manner in which he exalts the human ideal as the crown of all culture, he not only goes too far, but weakens the efficiency of his own contention, when he isolates humankind from the rest of nature as something wholly unrelated and apart. "There is nothing human," he says, "in any living animal. All Nature, the universe as far as we see, is anti- or ultra-human, outside, and has no concern with man." He thus places himself in direct antagonism to the general tendency of contemporary ethics no less than of contemporary science, being compelled to assert dogmatically on the one hand that "nothing is evolved, there is no evolution any more than there is design in Nature," and on the other to stand a'oof from that most beneficent and, in the truest sense, humanising spirit which more and more is leading us to regard mankind as sharers in a universal brotherhood of all living things.

And there is this obvious difficulty; why, if Nature is wholly ultra-human and indifferent, is communion with Nature so strongly advocated by Jefferies as the surest training for the soul? Why, to repeat his own words, do "all things seem possible in the open air"? To this question he gives no satisfactory answer; nor is it easy to see what answer can be given from his standpoint. "I was aware," he says, "that in reality the feeling and the thought were in me, and not in the earth or sun; yet I was more conscious of it when in company with these." But why, if there was no sympathy?

I have already noticed the contrast between Jefferies and Thoreau on the subject of man's relations with the lower animals. We largely miss in Jefferies the sense of natural brotherhood, and consequent magnetic sympathy with the inhabitants of field and forest, which Thoreau possessed in as great a measure as St. Francis, and which lend so singular a charm to the personality of the Walden philosopher. The hunting instinct was strong in Jefferies; in Thoreau it was well-nigh extinct. Take, for example, their respective mention of the hare. "The hare," says Thoreau, "in its extremity cries like a child; I warn you, mothers, that my sympathies do not always make the usual philanthropic distinctions." It is Jefferies' opinion that " hares are almost formed on purpose to be good sport." And so in numerous other instances; while the one thinker sees a sharp distinction between the human and the brute creation, the other expresses himself as " pathetically affected " by the human traits of animals, and surmises that among them, too, a civilisation may even now be progressing.

This defect on Jefferies' part is indicative of something more than a want of sympathy in a particular direction; his whole philosophy, if such it can be called, for indeed he is rather idealist than philosopher, is devoid of a solid rational foundation. By his absolute disregard of the past, and sweeping contempt for every doctrine of historical succession, he leaves no *locus standi* for his own individual personality, no logical starting-point for his own venturesome speculations. Triumphantly right as he often proves in his intellectual judgments, his success is due rather to his flashes of instinctive insight than to any trustworthy reliance on a connected train of reasoning. It is easy to condemn this mental isolation, easy even to ridicule it; but it is possible that herein lies the secret of much of Jefferies' strength, as also of many of his failings. The reckless mariner who cuts himself adrift from his moorings to run before the storm will in some cases get the earliest glimpse of an unknown shore.

This lack of firm basis and balance in Jefferies' intellectual system was doubtless due in some measure to the disadvantages of his personal isolation, and to the same cause, perhaps, may be ascribed the prejudices and dash of Philistinism that are observable here and there even in his later and better writings. He was never so dogmatic as on the subjects of which he knew least, such as thrift, hygiene, philanthropy, and other modern "quackeries," which, as his contemptuous references show, he had made no effort to appreciate or understand. In like manner his sarcasms on social anomalies sometimes lack point, because he had not sufficiently grasped the whole social position, but was speaking rather in the capacity of a disappointed or indifferent outsider.

I have said throughout that the key to Jefferies' character is to be sought in his rich sensuous disposition, full of passionate yearning for physical no less than spiritual beauty. His natural religion may be summed up in his own words: "I believe in the human being, mind and form, flesh and soul." He held it to be the sacred duty of every man and woman to cultivate, by all the means in their power, all possibilities of physical health, inasmuch as a deficiency in bodily vigour must inevitably warp and stunt the corresponding vigour of the soul. An idealist of this kind could hardly fail to resent and rebel against the sordid heartless conditions of modern society, in which half the grace and joy of living are strangled in the wolfish struggle of competitive existence. We are told by Mr. Besant that Jefferies "could never have called himself a socialist, but he sympathised with that part of socialism which claims for every man the full profit of the labour of his hands." There are many indications in his later volumes of his socialistic or rather communistic spirit, which is the more remarkable as having developed itself quite spontaneously from his own personality, in direct opposition to all the associations and surroundings of his youth and manhood.

It is interesting to note the process of this change. In his earliest writings on the agricultural question (which, by the way, are published in his latest posthumous volume, *The Toilers of the Field*, an incongruity which seems to have led some readers to mistake Jefferies' crudest judgments for his most mature ones) we find him the champion of the tenant-farmer against the labourer ; and it was in this capacity that he wrote, in 1872, those letters to *The Times*, on the subject of "The Wiltshire Labourer," which first brought him into public notice, *The Times* solemnly devoting a leader to enforce the moral of the letters, and to preach a thrifty self-reform to men who earned the magnificent wages of ten to thirteen shillings per week![1] In these juvenile essays there are many references to the mischief-making "agitators," "the teaching of the Radical papers," the "hatred which the Labourers' Union agents endeavour to sow between the labourer and the farmer," the "ingratitude" of the labouring classes, and all the usual platitudes of the conservative moralist. In emphasising the hardships of the tenant-farmer, Jefferies throughout speaks as if the farmer's only antagonist were the

---

[1] "Here, then, is that life of competency without care which poets dream of."—*The Times*, Nov. 14, 1872.

labourer; the landlord's share in the business is entirely overlooked and forgotten. Evidently the young yeoman-journalist had not at that time comprehended the central and governing fact of the position, although he was so well acquainted with the complexity of its details. He merely glorifies the farmer's cause as against the labourer, and adopts the farmer's creed, "I believe in the Sovereign, the Church, and the Land." The *landlord* is too sacred a personage to be mixed up in any sordid considerations of pounds, shillings, and pence.

Turn now to *The Dewy Morn*, one of the later of Jefferies' books (1884), and you will find an extraordinary contrast to the opinions of twelve years earlier, and even to those expressed in *Hodge and his Masters* (1880), where the landlord is represented as confronted on all sides "with unreasonable demands." The House of Cornleigh Cornleigh, Esq., the typical great landlord in the story, is subjected to merciless criticism; the serfdom of the labourer and the subservience of the tenant-farmer being clearly shown to be due to one and the same cause. "*Cornleigh Cornleigh, Esq., had got the land.*" There, in one pregnant sentence, has Jefferies summed up the situation. "The chief condition of cottage occupation," he says, "is that the cottager shall work for the farmer upon whose farm the cottage is situate. The moment any difference arises, the labourer has not only to leave his employment but his home. This, if he be a married man, generally means that he must leave the hamlet, because all the other cottages are full. The custom is the last relic of feudal times, for while this condition endures the labourer must still be a serf."

So, too, of his own class, the tenant-farmers: "Either bow the knee and touch the hat," he makes the landlords say; "vote as we please, give up your very conscience—either bow the knee and touch your hat, or leave your farm." "Oh, foolish House of Cornleigh!" he adds. "Foolish Houses of Cornleigh —very much in the plural, for they are a multitude in number—not to have made friends with Flesh and Blood, instead of grasping so blindly only at the mud underneath; neglecting and utterly ignoring the hearts that beat in the homesteads, laying hands so ambitiously on the mere surface of the earth."

If we are compelled to note a certain lack of sympathetic feeling in Jefferies' attitude towards the lower animals, we can claim on the other hand that no recent writer has more humanely and powerfully exposed the injustice, and furthermore the danger, of the harsh treatment accorded by society (as represented by official Bumbledom) to the agricultural poor.

"Modern civilisation has put out the spiritual devil and produced a devil of dynamite. Let me raise a voice in pleading for more humane treatment of the poor—the only way, believe me, by which society can narrow down and confine the operations of this new devil. A human being is not a dog, yet is treated worse than a dog. Force these human dogs to learn to read with empty stomachs—stomachs craving for a piece of bread while education is crammed into them. In manhood, if unfortunate, set them to break stones. If imbecility supervene, give them bread and water. In helpless age, give them the cup of cold water. This is the way to breed dynamite."[1]

The Poor Law, as at present administered, is repeatedly denounced by him in terms of unmeasured abhorrence. He characterises the application of the word "pauper" to any human being as "the greatest, the vilest, the most unpardonable crime that could be committed."

Charity organisation is similarly referred to as a "spurious, lying, false, and abominable mockery;" while it is his deliberate opinion that "the more philanthropy is talked about, and especially scientific philanthropy, the more individual suffering there is." Even in *Hodge and his Masters*, published as early as 1880, and written when Jefferies still believed that the agricultural labourer, as compared with the landowner, had "the best of the bargain," there is a terrible latent suggestiveness in the concluding chapter, which describes how the aged labourer, who has survived all his relatives and is unable to work any more, is removed at last from the cottage with which his whole life has been associated, to the workhouse in which he is a mere figure and machine.

"After all the ploughing and the sowing, the hoeing and the harvest, comes the miserable end. Strong as the labourer may be, thick-set and capable of immense endurance, by slow degrees that strength must

---

[1] "The Field Play," in *The Life of the Fields*.

wear away. The limbs totter, the back is bowed, the dimmed sight can no longer guide the plough in a straight furrow, nor the weak hands wield the reaping-hook. Hodge, who Atlas-like supported upon his shoulders the agricultural world, comes in his old age under the dominion of his last masters at the workhouse. . . . . . What amount of production did that old man's life of labour represent? What value must be put upon the labour of the son that fought in India; of the son that worked in Australia; of the daughter in New Zealand, whose children will help to build up a new nation? These things surely have their value. Hodge died; and the very gravedigger grumbled as he delved through the earth, hard-bound in the iron frost, for it jarred his hand and might break his spade. The low mound will soon be level, and the place of his burial shall not be known."

And these significant words were published in the *Standard*!

Nor was it only on such agricultural matters that Jefferies' views were revolutionised, for as regards the labour question in general he was in heart and feeling—however much he might have resented the name and association—a communist. He maintains, in a notable passage of his *Story*,[1] that a mere fraction of the heavy toil which men now undergo might, under a rational system of forethought and organisation, be sufficient to fill the whole world with abundance of comfort and happiness.

"This our earth produces not only a sufficiency, but a superabundance, and pours a cornucopia of

---

[1] Pp. 173, 174, second edition.

good things down upon us. Further, it produces sufficient for stores and granaries to be filled to the roof-tree for years a-head. I verily believe that the earth in one year produces enough food to last for thirty. Why, then, have we not enough? Why do people die of starvation, or lead a miserable existence on the verge of it? Why have millions upon millions to toil from morning to evening just to gain a mere crust of bread? Because of the absolute lack of organisation by which such labour should produce its effect, the absolute lack of distribution, the absolute lack even of the very idea that such things are possible. Nay, even to mention such things, to say that they are possible, is criminal with many. Madness could hardly go farther."

If anyone thinks that the above are mere isolated sentiments in Jefferies' writings, I would refer him to the striking extracts given in the *Pall Mall Gazette* (November 10, 1891), from some unpublished and fragmentary "Notes on the Labour Question." Here is Jefferies' opinion on the Divine Right of Capital:—

"This is the Divine Right of Capital. Look, the fierce sunshine beats down upon the white sand, or chalk, or hard clay of the railway cutting whose narrow sides focus the heat like a lens. Brawny arms swing the pick and drive the pointed spades into the soil. Clod by clod, inch by inch, the heavy earth is loosened, and the mountain removed by atoms at a time. Aching arms these, weary backs, stiffened limbs—brows black with dirt and perspiration. The glaring chalk blinds the eye with its whiteness; the slippery sand gives way beneath the footstep, or rises with the wind and fills the mouth with grit; the clay clings to the boot, weighing the leg down as lead.

The hot sun scorches the back of the neck—the lips grow dry and parched; and—'Look out for yourself, mate!' With a jarring rattle the clumsy trucks come jolting down the incline on their way to the 'shoot'; then beware, for they will sometimes jump the ill-laid track, and crush human limbs like brittle icicles with tons of earth. Or a 'shot' is fired overhead, bellowing as the roar rushes from cliff to cliff as an angry bull, and huge stones and fragments hurtle in deadly shower. Or, worse than all, the treacherous clay slips—bulges, trembles, and thuds in an awful avalanche, burying men alive.

"'But they are paid to do it,' says Comfortable Respectability (which hates everything in the shape of a 'question,' glad to slur it over somehow). They are paid to do it! Go down into the pit yourself, Comfortable Respectability, and try it as I have done, just one hour of a summer's day; then you will know the preciousness of a vulgar pot of beer! Three-and-sixpence a day is the price of these brawny muscles; the price of the rascally sherry you parade before your guests in such pseudo-generous profusion. One guinea a week—that is, one stall at the opera. But why do they do it? Because Hunger and Thirst drive them; these are the fearful scourges, the whips worse than the knout, which lie at the back of Capital and give it its power. Do you suppose these human beings with minds and souls and feelings would not otherwise repose on the sweet sward, and hearken to the song-birds as you may do on your lawn at Cedar Villa?

"The 'financier,' 'director,' 'contractor,' whatever his commercial title—perhaps all three, who is floating this line, where is he? Rolling in his carriage right royally as a King of Spades should do, honoured for the benefits he has conferred upon mankind, toasted at banquets, knighted by an appreciative Throne, his lady shining in bright raiment by his side, glorious in silk and scarlet and ermine, smiling as her lord, voluble of speech, pours forth his unctuous harangue. One man whipped with Hunger toils half-naked in the Pit, face to face with death; the other is crowned by his fellows, sitting in state with fine wines and the sound of jubilee. This is the Divine Right of Capital."

Let us now turn to the subject of Jefferies' views on religion. Here, too, we find the same complete change from the opinions of his youth, for whereas he was at first of the strictly orthodox persuasion, and his early letters, as his biographer tells us, are full of a boyish piety, he afterwards arrived at the conclusion that a disbelief in a directing intelligence is the necessary starting-point for every sort of progression. "In the march of time," he says in a notable passage of the *Story*, "there fell away from my mind, as the leaves from the trees in autumn, the last traces and relics of superstitions and traditions acquired compulsorily in childhood. Always feebly adhering, they finally disappeared."

In summarising Jefferies' creed, I follow without hesitation the account deliberately given in his autobiography; because, for reasons presently to be stated,[1] I do not attach much importance to the story of his subsequent return to the Christian faith. In view, however, of the controversy that has arisen about his alleged death-bed conversion, it is necessary to point out that Jefferies' atheism (or pantheism, if the term be preferred) was at no time *materialistic*; he simply

---

[1] See Note at end of this Chapter.

exchanged the orthodox belief, which had never satisfied his higher instincts, for a natural religion which was entirely in harmony with his whole spiritual being. In his own terse but eloquent expression—" with disbelief belief increased." It is therefore wholly meaningless to argue that a man of so profoundly religious a nature could not have remained an "unbeliever"; the sole question is—of what did his belief consist? And on this point there is positively no room for doubt.

As regards the past and future of the human race, Jefferies' doctrines are a strange mixture of despondency and hopefulness; disbelieving in those assurances to which most men cling, he draws from this disbelief a reason for strength and confidence. He is under no delusions, he says, as to the insecurity of religious faith; he believes in no over-ruling intelligence; he finds no trace of the existence of a deity, either in nature or in human affairs. Nay, more, he considers that it is a falsehood and a crime against humanity to assert that all things happen for some beneficent end, since "the whole and the worst the worst pessimist can say is far beneath the least particle of the truth, so immense is the misery of man." The question of the soul's immortality is one which, in our present limited range of ideas, can be answered neither in the affirmative nor negative—the future, if there be a future, is beyond our ken. This, however, is no cause for despair, but rather for hope, since the moment we recognise that there is no directing intelligence, but that man is left to himself and free to become master of his own destinies, we at once have a rational motive for energy and self-improvement. The certainty of death, and the uncertainty of the future beyond it, are urgent injunctions on mankind to dispel their superstitious illusions and to realise the supreme importance of the present life, since by a resolute effort now we may pave the way for the happiness of future generations. What this happiness shall be we can only surmise, but Jefferies hints at the possibility of a perfection which transcends all present belief. "All diseases," he says, "without exception are preventable. All accidents are crimes." So potent is human thought, so infinite its scope, that things now deemed supernatural may yet prove to be discoverable, and man may enter on an exalted and spiritualised existence from which even death itself may be eliminated. But the first and most absolutely necessary step is the rejection of superstitious belief, for it is by this that human effort has hitherto been paralysed.

It is a complete, though very common error, to call a thinker who holds such a creed as this a "pessimist," inasmuch as with the very recognition of present failure he combines a strong assurance of future success. "Full well aware," he says, "that all has failed, yet, side by side with the sadness of that knowledge, there lives on in me an unquenchable belief, thought burning like the sun, that there is yet something to be found, something real, something to give each separate personality sunshine and flowers in its own existence now." If this be pessimism, it is a pessimism of a very strange and self-destructive kind.

Yet it would be futile to deny that there are times and moods in which the effect of Jefferies' writings is disheartening and depressing to the reader. I quote the following from the letter of an American friend and correspondent :—

"On Sunday last I strolled into the depths of a quiet forest, and laid myself down on the sward under a beech tree, and there read *The Story of my Heart.* When I arose to go home, the shadows were long and grey, and the silence was beyond the power of words to describe. I had lain on the grass thinking after I had finished the book, and between the scene, the silence and the book, I felt as I have never felt before. The mystery of existence filled me, and to every question that I asked my soul there came no reply—there was only the awful silence. In all my life I have never had an hour of such utter desolation of soul. I could find in myself no resignation to the inexorable mystery; I felt that it was even cruel to leave us so wholly in the dark, and I was filled with a sullen defiance. That night I could not rest: the book was ever recurring and bringing up the problem."

The key to a seeming contradiction lies in the fact that Jefferies' spiritual and intellectual hopes, like those of Shelley, were centred on the future—a future which he knew to be a remote, perhaps immeasurably remote one, but which he also knew to be as certain as to-morrow's dawn. For just as his mind had "felt back" through the centuries until the dead were real to him as the living, so also had it felt forward through the centuries until the future became by sympathy the present, and he was enabled to look with equanimity on the ruin of individual success. A man of this nature must necessarily live a life of seclusion. In the present officious age of propagandism and proselytism, and philanthropic concern for one's own and other people's souls, he had little or no part. He was a pagan, a pantheist, a worshipper of earth and sea, and of the great sun " burning in the heaven "; he yearned for a free, natural, fearless life of physical health and spiritual exaltation, and for a death in harmony with the life that preceded it.

With a full sense of Jefferies' defects as a thinker, defects which I have not attempted to palliate or minimise, I believe there are few ideals in modern days more worthy of the attention of a sophisticated and artificial society than that plea for a return to nature which is the first and last word of his gospel.

NOTE.

THE CONVERSION OF RICHARD JEFFERIES.

The alarming discovery was made two years ago by an ingenuous correspondent of the *Pall Mall Gazette*, that Richard Jefferies, the prose-poet of natural history, not content with the legitimate study of game-keepers and poachers, had made a most reprehensible incursion into the domain of theology, by setting forth in an obscure volume entitled *The Story of my Heart*, the outrageous opinion that "there is not the least trace of directing intelligence in human affairs." The discoverer of this outrage, being quite innocent of any familiar knowledge of Jefferies' life or writings, which would have afforded proof that he was, in the best and only true sense, a profoundly religious man, naturally felt called upon to address a letter to the papers ; and the result was a correspondence, first on the subject of " The Pernicious Works of Richard Jefferies," and then on the supplementary question, " Did Richard Jefferies die a Christian ? "

For it is argued by Jefferies' orthodox admirers that though he did indeed " hold sceptical opinions for a time," as expressed in the heretical *Story of my Heart*, he nevertheless died in the full odour of piety, and would probably, had he survived, have withdrawn the offending autobiography from circulation, or at least have added a later chapter with a wholly different conclusion—just as it was suggested by Nathaniel Hawthorne, in one of his finest moods of irony, that Shelley, if he had lived to a ripe age, would have taken holy orders, and been "inducted to a small country living in the gift of the lord chancellor."

But in spite of the "authoritative account of the closing scene," which the *Pall Mall Gazette* reprinted from that very suitable repository, the columns of the *Girls' Own Paper* (to think that ' *visi puellis nuper idoneus* ' should be said of Richard Jefferies !) I greatly question whether he can be said to have died a Christian, even in the most superficial sense, for it is incredible that a man of his progressive intellect should have gone back to a creed which he had once conscientiously held, but had gradually outgrown and abandoned. In 1883, four years before his death, but when the prospect of death was already familiar to him, he wrote as follows in the final chapter of *The Story of my Heart* :

" I have been obliged to write these things by an irresistible impulse which has worked in me since early youth. They have not been written for the sake of argument, still less for any thought of profit, rather indeed the reverse. They have been forced from me by earnestness of heart, and they express my most serious convictions. For seventeen years they have been lying in my mind, continually thought of and pondered over."

It is evident from this and other similar passages in the book, that in *The Story of my Heart* we have Jefferies' intellectual will and testament, drawn up, at what he felt to be the close of his active career, with the utmost solemnity and deliberation. Note further that the same free-thinking views were again expressed and emphasised in "Hours of Spring," an essay which appeared in *Longman's* as late as May, 1886, that is, only fifteen months before the death of the writer. We may regard it, therefore, as beyond doubt that the change in Jefferies' convictions, if change there were, took place within the last year of his life.

Now, when we take into consideration the terribly shattered state of his health at the end, it is surprising that any importance should be attributed to such a conversion, or that orthodox people should derive any gratification from being told that a man broken by disease, poverty-stricken, solitary, devoid of all intellectual companionship, died "listening with faith and love to the words contained in the Old Book,"— a book with which, as we know, he had been intimately familiar from boyhood. We are reminded of James Thomson's remark about the "convertites" of Kingsley's novels, that "Mr. Kingsley brings in these miserable wrecks and relics of what were once men and women as all that he can contribute to the extension of the Church, which ought to be the cheerful congregation of wholesome men and women throughout the world." Moreover, the very facts of a case of this kind are extremely unreliable when they depend on the sole evidence of those who, by their own showing, were deeply concerned to produce a particular result, for such persons are dangerously apt to exaggerate trifles unintentionally, to see an undue significance in chance words and speeches, and to hail as the desired spiritual change that which is in reality nothing more than complete bodily collapse.

Herein is the simple explanation of Jefferies' alleged conversion. He was very weak—so weak that he perhaps could not but yield outward acquiescence to the affectionate importunities of those around him, while still inwardly holding the views which, as he recently avowed, "expressed his most serious convictions." So long as he retained any slight measure of health and strength, so long as he was able, even at rare intervals, to enjoy that vital communion with Nature on which his whole being depended, so long in fact as he was Richard Jefferies, and not a shattered wreck—he was a free-thinker. Even at the last he withdrew no syllable of his writings; he saw no priest; he made no acceptance of any sort of dogma. His own published statements remain, and will remain, beyond dispute or question the authoritative expression of his life-creed.

V.—AS WRITER.

THE quality of Richard Jefferies' literary style, as of his personal temperament, was rich, sensuous, lavish, diffuse. The close correspondence of style with thought—of the external expression with the inner meaning—is very marked in Jefferies; and the merits and defects of each stage of his intellectual development may be as clearly traced in the manner as in the substance of his writings. Having seen how the rather commonplace young reporter was gradually transformed into the devoted enthusiast and nature student, we shall be prepared to find a proportionate difference of value between the workmanship of such a novel as (let us say) *The Scarlet Shawl* and that of such an essay as "The Pageant of Summer."

I do not propose to dwell at any length on the literary aspects of Jefferies' *juvenilia*, for a detailed study would here be as unnecessary as in the case of the various petty incidents recorded of his early life. There is really nothing to be said of such works as the *Memoir of the Goddards*, or *The Scarlet Shawl*, or the pamphlet *Jack Brass*, except that they are entirely dull and uninteresting, and show no promise whatever of literary or intellectual ability. On the other hand, the early essays on agricultural subjects contributed to

The Times, Fraser's Magazine, and the *New Quarterly* (a more numerous series than most of Jefferies' readers are aware of), are greatly superior in every way to the novels and pamphlets of the same period, and have just so much real merit as belongs to a clear practical statement of matters with which the writer was himself personally familiar; but they are not in any sense literature, and it is open to question if they are now worth collecting and reprinting in permanent form. It is certainly to be hoped that the growing interest in Jefferies' personality will not lead, as in Shelley's case, to a resuscitation of all the poor stuff which he perpetrated in the innocence of his boyhood; but even now there are ominous signs that the book-collector is on the war-path, and engaged in his congenial task of assigning a fictitious value to productions that are essentially valueless. Already someone has apparently found it worth his while to "mislay" from the British Museum the very dull, though scarce, little handbook on *Reporting, Editing, and Authorship,* and another to forge copies of the pamphlet entitled *Suez-cide.* Of Jefferies' so-called novels, some of which are found in each period of his authorship, it will be more convenient to speak presently as a whole.

In his mature style, as in his mature thought, two main phases are observable. The "Sketches of Natural History and Rural Life"—a sub-title which is applicable not to the *Gamekeeper* only, but to all the series of writings published between 1877 and 1881— are expressed in language which is at once simple, serviceable, and artistic, with now and again a touch of that deeper suggestiveness which is mostly of a later growth. Nothing could be better in their way than the country pictures so carefully and tenderly drawn for us by Jefferies the naturalist, as, for example, the following description of the old-fashioned waggon in *Wild Life*.

"For, like a ship, the true old-fashioned waggon is full of curves, and there is scarcely a straight piece of wood about it. Nothing is angular or square; and each piece of timber, too, is carved in some degree, bevelled at the edges, the sharp outline relieved in one way or another, and the whole structure like a ship, seeming buoyant, and floating, as it were, easily on the wheels. Then the painting takes several weeks, and after that the lettering of the name ; and when at last completed it is placed outside by the road, that every farmer and labourer who goes by may pause and admire. In about twelve months, if the builder be expeditious (for him), the new vessel may reach her port under the open shed at the farm, and then her life of voyages begins. . . . .

"How many a man's life has centred about the waggon ! As a child he rides in it as a treat to the hay-field with his father; as a lad he walks beside the leader, and gets his first ideas of the great world when they visit the market town. As a man he takes command and pilots the ship for many a long, long year. When he marries, the waggon, lent for his own use, brings home his furniture. After a while his own children go for a ride in it, and play in it when stationary in the shed. In the painful ending the waggon carries the weak-kneed old man in pity to and from the old town for his weekly store of goods, or mayhap for his weekly dole of that staff of life his aged teeth can hardly grind. And many a plain coffin has the old waggon carried to the distant churchyard on the side of the hill. It is a cold spot—as life, too, was cold and hard ; yet in the spring the daisies will come, and the thrushes will sing on the bough."

Few readers could fail to appreciate such writing as this. Indeed it may be fairly said of all this portion of Jefferies' labours that *it has its reward*. The fact that he is already accepted in some degree as a classic—that he is not, even at the present time, six years after his death, unknown to any but the inner circle of his admirers—is due to the well-deserved popularity of *Wild Life* and its fellow-volumes. I have in a previous chapter stated my reasons for believing that this preference, though natural and inevitable now, can only be a temporary one; nevertheless it is an actual preference, which has to be admitted and reckoned with. We have, therefore, this highly anomalous state of affairs—that whereas Jefferies' real and ultimate fame as a writer is based on his later and more imaginative essays, his present commercial-literary reputation is based on an antecedent, transitional, and distinctly subordinate phase of workmanship. He survives in booksellers' catalogues as the author of *The Gamekeeper at Home*, that he may be known to future ages as the author of *The Story of my Heart*.

For let us be under no mistake on this point. It was as poet-naturalist, not as naturalist merely, that Jefferies attained to a true literary mastership, and he will finally be judged as a writer by the work done during his last six years. And here, it must be admitted, he is for the present at a disadvantage; for not only is the average reader (and perhaps it must be added the average literary man) quite unable to relish the peculiar and subtle quality by which Jefferies, no less than Thoreau, is distinguished; but furthermore the faults which lie on the surface of Jefferies' later and idealistic utterances are as obvious and unmistakable as the merits of his earlier style. Everybody can see the beauties of his simple, faithful delineations of English country life; everybody can see the blemishes inseparable from his attempts to express the deeper and more complex emotions of the soul; but not everybody can feel the extraordinary charm of Jefferies at his highest—the magic of such inimitable masterpieces as " Hours of Spring " or " The Pageant of Summer." For the present, Jefferies in the finest efforts of his genius is necessarily for the few. Let us be thankful that the many are content to do him homage for sufficient reasons of their own.

I am fully aware that Jefferies' characteristic mannerisms of laxity and over-diffuseness, and his tendency to a shambling, slipshod, "cataloguing" style, grew worse and more incorrigible in a considerable proportion of his later writings, and that good, bad, and indifferent are inartistically mixed together in the four volumes of his collected essays;[1] but this is amply accounted for by the fact that he was more and more compelled by sheer stress of poverty to write what was immediately acceptable for journalistic purposes,

---

[1] *Nature near London; The Life of the Fields; The Open Air; Field and Hedgerow.*

and to republish the same in volume form for the sake of getting the utmost value from his work. It has been said that he was no artist, having no faculty of selection; that his work is not a picture, but "a long-drawn sequence of statements," and that he was merely "bent on emptying his note-book in decent English."[1] It cannot be denied that there is some truth in these strictures, as applied to a part of Jefferies' work, though by no means to all of it, for a more unequal writer never gave himself away to unfriendly critics. But how absurd is this, that a general and sweeping sentence should thus be passed on an author, without regard to the inequalities caused by the hard conditions of his life! We must judge a man by his best work, and not by his indifferent work, unless we are aforehand determined to come to a wrong conclusion about him; and each of the four volumes to which reference has been made contains essays fit to be ranked with the very finest of Jefferies' productions.

It may, however, be justly charged against him that there are some ugly solecisms scattered here and there in his volumes, and that his habit of adding explanatory dissertations to his remarks on outdoor life—accrescent layers of information sandwiched in between patches of narrative—is sometimes very trying to the patience of his readers. His desultory and discursive habit was inveterate and constitutional, and shows itself both in the subject and the form of his writings. Take as an example his account of how

---

[1] *Athenæum*, December 8, 1888.

one of his friends was chased by bucks as he was bicycling through a forest—an incident which is interpolated in a chapter devoted to stoats and birds,[1] and is, as Jefferies gravely remarks, "a little outside his subject." A sense of humour would have saved him from many such lapses into an irrelevant and tedious wordiness; but unfortunately humour was not one of his characteristics. Sarcastic he could be, and scathingly ironical at times; but of humour there is hardly a trace in the whole series of his volumes. That all his native faults of temperament—his desultory moodiness, his dogmatism and lack of humour—are frequently, at times painfully, reflected in his style, will not be denied by the most appreciative and enthusiastic of his admirers.

On the other hand the fact remains that the inherent excellence of his literary style, although for the present appreciated only by the few, is of far more importance than the incidental and superficial blemishes. He is one of the small number, the very small number, of great prose writers of his generation. He is a master of "prose-poetry;" and prose-poetry, it is worth observing, is quite another thing, and a more valuable thing, than poets' prose.[2] It is by no means rare for a poetical prose of high quality to be produced by poets—the works of Shelley and James

---

[1] *Round about a Great Estate*, p. 58.

[2] I advisedly use the expression "prose-poetry," although I am aware that some critics condemn it as a contradiction in terms. The proper antithesis, I think, is not between prose and poetry, but between prose and verse. Poetry is found in both verse and prose.

Thomson furnish signal instances of this—yet in such cases we usually feel that the prose, however beautiful, is merely the counterpart of the poetry, instead of being the most spontaneous and unmistakable expression of the writer's genius. But in great and genuine prose-poetry, such as the dream-fugues of De Quincey, there is an elemental and impressive energy which carries its own credentials; it is not a brilliant variation from a more characteristic mode of writing, but a style, a tone, an achievement in itself. It is by merit of this possession of an original and distinctive style that Jefferies can claim the rank of a great prose writer.

For if the limitations of Jefferies' personality are reproduced in his writings, so also, and in far larger measure, are its great and generous features reproduced there—above all, the passion, and the purity in passion, by which he is conspicuously distinguished. Of all the mistaken judgments pronounced on him by reviewers, perhaps the most mistaken is the assertion that his work is devoid of "the passionate human interest."[1] A white heat of passionate feeling, as pure as it is fervid, everywhere underlies and inspires the best of his later essays; despite the outward calmness of the language, no sympathetic reader (and what criticism can be discerning unless it be sympathetic?) will overlook the intensity of the human interest that is dominant throughout. We have seen how the Wiltshire rustics, his neighbours at Coate, were but litt'e impressed by the spectacle of the youthful natu-

---

[1] *Athenæum*, Dec. 8, 1888.

ralist absorbed in reverie on the hill-top, and Jefferies himself has remarked that no one would have imagined the "whirlwind of passion" that was going on within him as he reclined there. It is to be regretted that the critics should give a similar but less pardonable exhibition of bucolic insensibility; for to fail to appreciate the beauty of Jefferies' prose-poems is positively not a matter for self-satisfaction.

As a master of language he is equalled, at his best, by few contemporary writers, and surpassed by fewer still, so perfectly melodious are his sentences, so full of tender gravity, so simple yet so subtle in their structure and modulation. Monotonous his style may be, but only as the burden of a rippling stream is monotonous, lapsing on from thought to thought in harmonious sequence. Moreover, Jefferies is a great lover of the refrain. Like his favourite harbinger of summer warmth, the swallow, which from its circling, haunting flight has been named by another poet-naturalist *l'oiseau du retour*, it is his habit to haunt and circle round and revisit some special phrase or cadence, whose repetition may serve as a suggestive undertone to his melody.

Jefferies' resemblance to Shelley, of which I have once or twice made mention, is something more than a mere coincidence in manner, for in several respects the two idealists were naturally and constitutionally akin. It cannot be said that Jefferies' life was lived on so high a plane as Shelley's, yet we note in him the same ardent sanguine temperament to which, in spite of the crushing tyranny of present evils, a firm faith in the equality and perfectibility of mankind was a constant source of inspiration; the same extraordinary sensitiveness to the quickening influences of nature; the same "golden purity" of feeling and thought, confused at first in the turbid ambitions of restless youth, and vainly striving to image itself in wild and impossible romances, but in the end clarified and tranquillised in a style where it might seem that the words, as has been said of Shelley's words, "were really transparent, or that they throbbed with living lustres"—there is such crystalline brilliancy, and withal a heart of fire, both in the idea and in the expression.

There is no doubt that judged from a literary as well as from an intellectual standpoint, the most noteworthy of Jefferies' complete volumes is *The Story of my Heart*. Of the shorter essays, the two best and most characteristic, in my opinion, are "The Pageant of Summer"—that wonderful rhapsody aglow with all the fire of Jefferies' idealism—and "Hours of Spring," in which the contrary picture of wintry desolation is enforced with terrible directness. To those who would rightly understand the sunshine and the shadow, the mingled vein of hopefulness and despondency, that ran through Jefferies' temperament, I would recommend a comparative study of these two masterpieces. Only a brief quotation from each is here permissible.

"It is in this marvellous transformation of clods and cold matter into living things that the joy and the hope of summer reside. Every blade of grass, each leaf, each separate floret and petal, is an inscription speaking of hope. Consider the grasses and the oaks, the swallows, the sweet blue butterfly—they are one and all a sign and token showing before our eyes earth made into life. So that my hope becomes as broad as the horizon afar, reiterated by every leaf, sung on every bough, reflected in the gleam of every flower. There is so much for us yet to come, so much to be gathered and enjoyed. Not for you or me now, but for our race, who will ultimately use this magical secret for their happiness. Earth holds secrets enough to give them the life of the fabled Immortals. My heart is fixed firm and stable in the belief that ultimately the sunshine and the summer, the flowers and the azure sky, shall become, as it were, interwoven into man's existence."[1]

"For weeks and weeks the stark black oaks stood straight out of the snow as masts of ships with furled sails frozen and ice-bound in the haven of the deep valley. Each was visible to the foot, set in the white slope, made individual in the wood by the brilliance of the background. Never was such a long winter. For fully two months they stood in the snow in black armour of iron bark unshaken, the front rank of the forest army that would not yield to the northern invader. Snow in broad flakes, snow in semi-flakes, snow raining down in frozen specks, whirling and twisting in fury, ice raining in small shot of frost, howling, sleeting, groaning; the ground like iron, the sky black and faintly yellow—brutal colours of despotism—heaven striking with clenched fist. . . . . . No kindness to man from birth-hour to ending; neither earth, sky, nor gods care for him, innocent at the mother's breast. Nothing good to man but man. Let man, then, leave his gods and lift up his ideal beyond them."[2]

[1] "The Pageant of Summer," in *The Life of the Fields*.
[2] "Hours of Spring," in *Field and Hedgerow*.

As a final specimen of Jefferies' most poignant mood the following spring picture may be quoted, from the essay on "Wild Flowers" in *The Open Air*.

"A friend said, 'Why do you go the same road every day? Why not have a change and walk somewhere else sometimes? Why keep on up and down the same place?' I could not answer; till then it had not occurred to me that I did always go one way; as for the reason of it, I could not tell; I continued in my own mind while the summers went away. Not till years afterwards was I able to see why I went the same round and did not care for change. I do not want change; I want the same old and loved things, the same wild flowers, the same trees and soft ash-green; the turtle-doves, the blackbirds, the coloured yellow-hammer, sing, sing, singing so long as there is light to cast a shadow on the dial, for such is the measure of his song. and I want them in the same place. Let me find them morning after morning, the starry-white petals radiating, striving upwards to their ideal. Let me see the idle shadows resting on the white dust; let me hear the humble-bees, and stay to look down on the rich dandelion disk. Let me see the very thistles opening their great crowns—I should miss the thistles; the reed-grasses hiding the moor-hen; the bryony bine, at first crudely ambitious and lifted by force of youthful sap straight above the hedgerow to sink of its own weight presently and progress with crafty tendrils; swifts shot through the air with outstretched wings like crescent-headed, shaftless arrows darted from the clouds; the chaffinch with a feather in her bill; all the living staircase of the spring, step by step, upwards to the great gallery of the summer—let me watch the same succession year by year."

Turning from country to town, we find another

special characteristic of Jefferies the poet-naturalist in the spiritual glamour with which he clothes objects the most materialistic and commonplace, herein reminding us of Lucretius among ancient writers, and of Shelley and Whitman among modern. The great elemental forces of Nature are omnipresent and alive to him, not mere subjects of study and observation; even when he is treating of such scenes as would usually be considered most uncongenial to the poetical sense—as, for example, a modern south-coast watering-place—the nature-spirit is felt through it all. Witness this description of the King's Road at Brighton.

"The wind coming up the cliff seems to bring with it whole armfuls of sunshine, and to throw the warmth and light against you as you linger. The walls and glass reflect the light, and push back the wind in puffs and eddies; the awning flutters; light and wind spring upwards from the pavement; the sky is richly blue against the parapets overhead; there are houses on one side, but on the other open space and sea, and dim clouds in the extreme distance. The atmosphere is full of light, and gives a sense of liveliness; every atom of it is in motion."[1]

I have already quoted some typical passages from Jefferies' London essays. It is much to be regretted that he did not write more in that vein, but the reason is obvious—he was compelled for the most part to defer to the wishes of editors and publishers in the selection of his themes, and the country was found to

---

[1] "Sunny Brighton," in *The Open Air*.

yield a better profit than the town. *The Story of my Heart* was as distinctly a financial failure as the *Gamekeeper* was a success. It is curious to note that the reviewers, as representatives of the public, began latterly to take Jefferies to task for the "lack of variety" in his nature-studies, whereas when he *did* strike a new note they mostly failed to understand it! He thus had to undergo that critical process, severely trying even to the strongest characters, of being highly praised for his mediocre work and slighted for his masterpieces.

On the other hand the critics were undoubtedly justified in refusing to take him seriously in the capacity of novelist. It is difficult to come to any other conclusion than that he turned to the novel, in the first instance, because it is popularly supposed to be the most lucrative form of literature, and not from any very imperious inclination to the study of character. It is true that he at first possessed a certain youthful fluency in the weaving of romantic narratives, and that, as he informed a publisher, to write a tale was as easy to him as to write a letter. But then, as it happened, both his early tales and his early letters were of a very third-rate quality; so that it is a positive relief to his readers to find that in his later volumes this fatal fluency had altogether disappeared, and that he was compelled to have recourse to another faculty which is wholly unrelated to novel writing. In brief, he was an essayist, and not a novelist at all, nor under any circumstances could he have become a novelist. Even when he was well equipped with material, he was quite unable to give any vivid dramatic life to his stories.

I cannot, however, agree with Mr. Besant's statement, made in partial explanation of Jefferies' failure as a novelist, that "he knew nothing of society, nothing of men and women, except the people of a small country town." The series of articles on agricultural life, written by him between the age of twenty-five and thirty, shows a really surprising knowledge of interesting and valuable facts—valuable to anyone who had the capacity for using them to advantage. But Jefferies had not that capacity; his instinct was that of the naturalist who observes and moralises rather than of the novelist who penetrates and interprets; and consequently his rustic characters, though strongly and clearly drawn, do not live, as for example those of Thomas Hardy live. He could sympathise profoundly with human nature in general, but not with the individual man; uncommunicative himself, he was incapable of divining and portraying the emotions of others.

But this same incapacity, be it noted, affected his studies of animals scarcely less than his studies of men, and it is a mistake to suppose that he was uniformly successful when writing of the lower races, and uniformly unsuccessful when writing of human-kind. It is true that he has been praised by a discerning critic for the "world of animal life" depicted in his *Wood Magic* and *Bevis*, in which works, according to the same authority, he "fortunately felt a call to combine the novelist with the naturalist." But, after all, these fabulous representations of birds and beasts as imbued with human motives and human sentiments are a work rather of a lively fancy than a creative insight. His character-sketches of men are just as realistic and externally faithful as his descriptions of animals, and the only reason why they are less appreciated is that the public is least critical where it is most ignorant, and knowing nothing of animal life is apt to regard any knowledge of that subject as almost miraculous. But as for constructing a *story* from such material, Jefferies could do it as little in one case as in the other, and this for the same reason in both cases, that he had no dramatic power; men and animals are alike mere figures in his landscapes.

Nay more, his landscapes themselves show traces of the same deficiency, for, as a rule, he fails to give coherence and unity to his scenes. Even "Jefferies-land" does not impress itself on the reader's mental vision in the way that White's "Selborne" does; it is too vague and disconnected, a series of brilliant pictures, but not a dramatic whole. To *Red Deer* and one or two other works where greater concentration was inevitable this criticism does not apply.

Inasmuch, then, as Jefferies was not born a novelist, and the novelist's craft (witness the countless terrible evidences on the shelves of our circulating libraries) is not to be artificially acquired, it is somewhat comical to find him complaining, like a bad workman of his tools, of the novel as a form of literature. The novel, it seems, is but a clumsy and inefficient instrument as

---

[1] Dr. R. Garnett in *National Dictionary of Biography*.

compared with the drama—such at least is the avowed opinion of the author of *The Dewy Morn*, though he omits to explain why, if that be so, he did not come before us as a dramatist. "It occurred to me," he says, "how happy the dramatist must be, since he places his hero and his heroine in living shape at once before you. . . . The unfortunate narrator is not permitted these advantages. It takes me pages upon pages to describe a single character, and then very probably you do not see half what I had hoped you would see. . . . My arm and hand very often ache with the labour of writing just to explain the simplest set of circumstances, which upon the stage would not have been thought of. They would be taken for granted. This is very hard upon me, I think. Could you not let me write my scenes one after the other, and supply the connecting links out of your own imagination, as you do on the stage?"

It's extraordinary that Jefferies should have been so wholly unaware that the failure was in himself, and that his entire lack of dramatic instinct—not to mention his lack of humour—must have disqualified him even more for the drama than for the novel. And as for taking his scenes discontinuously, "one after the other," that is indeed the very method which readers are compelled to adopt, if his so-called novels are to be studied with any sort of satisfaction, such "connecting links" as he himself supplied being without either solidity or cohesion.

His later stories are far more readable than his earlier, not only on account of the general development of his powers, but also because he more and more ceased to trouble himself in the construction of a plot, and was content to ramble on from scene to scene and give free play to his individuality. The merit of these "novels" is thus enhanced by the fact that they are not narratives at all, but a series of splendid word-pictures, steeped in the richest colouring of their author's glowing imagination. "In the ordinary sense of the word," says Mr. Besant, "Jefferies was not a novelist; in the artistic sense of the word, he was not a novelist. This fully understood and conceded, we can afterwards consider his later so-called novels as so many storehouses filled with priceless treasure."

In none, I think, is this treasure so lavishly manifested as in *The Dewy Morn*, where, in the character of Felise, the heroine, we have an embodiment of the free, rich, voluptuous, yet sane and wholesome loveliness which Jefferies held so sacred. With the exception, perhaps, of Bevis, the boy-hero of *Wood Magic*, Felise is the only living personage whom Jefferies has drawn; we realise her far more clearly than the somewhat commonplace young ladies of *Green Ferne Farm*, more than the winsome but rather weakly-drawn Amaryllis, more than the saintly but shadowy Aurora in *After London;* she lives in our minds by force of her splendid physical beauty, her strong pure love, and her sweet happy mixture of simplicity and fearlessness. "Her natural body had been further perfected by a purely natural life. The wind, the sun, the fields, the hills—freedom and the spirit which dwells among these, had made her a natural woman; such a woman as Earth meant to live upon her surface, and as Earth intended in the first origin of things; beauty and strength — strength and beauty." None of Jefferies' pictures are purer or more impassioned than those in *The Dewy Morn*, such as the descriptions of Felise ascending the high slopes of the Downs, or swimming in the waters of the lake, or watching in the early summer morning by the side of her sleeping lover.

A few words remain to be said about the attitude of the literary profession towards Jefferies and his writings. It must be confessed, I think, that Jefferies has met with scant appreciation from the critics; not that there was any lack of laudatory press notices of his volumes, for it became the fashion to praise him, in his capacity of naturalist, as a sort of modern Gilbert White, but his more serious claims to a permanent place in our literature, have, with a few exceptions, been rather coldly received. Nor is this to be wondered at; for Jefferies, like Thoreau and other men of genius who have a message to their age, was not likely to be comprehended on an off-hand survey by versatile writers, who, (on the "repairs-done-while-you-wait" principle,) complacently unconscious that a judgment which is not based on familiarity or sympathy with its subject is worth precisely nothing, deliver a ready opinion on everything that comes within their ken.

Such critical blunders have been especially noticeable with regard to that nature-school to which

Jefferies belonged. Never was criticism more wildly wide of the mark than Matthew Arnold's high-and-mighty utterances on Shelley, or Lowell's malicious misrepresentations of Thoreau, or a recent unhappy defamation of Walt Whitman; indeed, to look over back numbers of literary reviews, with reference to any great nature student, is like re-reading old meteorological "forecasts"—we know not whether to marvel more at the infatuated assurance or the incorrigible blindness of the oracle. Thus, in the contemporary criticisms on Jefferies, it was magisterially asserted[1] that his *Red Deer*—an excellent monograph on Somersetshire stag-hunting, which is just what it purports to be, and no more—is likely "to live and be remembered when a score of such harmless, unnecessary exercises as *The Story of my Heart* are forgotten;" while another writer expressed the opinion that "Mr. Jefferies has not told the story of his own heart so well as he told the story of the Gamekeeper at Home or the Amateur Poacher," and further, that "there is really little heart or human interest in it . . . there is little pleading in his plea for 'soul-life'—it is brag."[2] This is the sort of thing that Jefferies had to accept as the judgment of his fellow-craftsmen on the highest efforts of his genius. There is evidently some truth in the remark of a great living writer, that "to publish is to have a dreadful illumination of the nature of one's countrymen."

It is by no means surprising that an author of

---

[1] *Athenæum*, February 9, 1884.
[2] *Academy*, November 3, 1883.

Jefferies' very unaccommodating and uncompromising temper should have so wholly failed, in spite of his literary powers, to attain a due commercial success. The story of his long struggle with poverty and ill-health is a dark and lamentable one; yet it is surely worse than futile to regret that this proudest and most sensitive of men, who in his extremest difficulties would not apply for help to the Royal Literary Fund because he regarded such patronage as an insult to his profession, was not, as Mr. Besant puts it, "adopted and tenderly nursed by some rich man." The Dean of Salisbury in his oration on Jefferies[1] expressed a similar wish that "there had been someone like the great Edmund Burke, who appeared as a good genius at the most critical time of the poet Crabbe's career, to lead and console a sorely tried spirit in the way to health, success, and fame." Imagine Richard Jefferies residing with Disraeli at Beaconsfield, as Crabbe did with Burke, and persuaded by his benefactor, as Crabbe was persuaded, to take holy orders by way of improving his prospects! But Jefferies' character was not like that of Crabbe; and the "good genius" who should have attempted to approach him as a patron would have early discovered his mistake.

But in spite of all obstacles, Jefferies' literary influence is a real and growing one. It is a trifling indication in itself, but a genuine tribute to the efficiency of his work, that he has been the founder of

---

[1] At the unveiling of the memorial in Salisbury Cathedral, March 9, 1892.

a popular *rus-in-urbe* school of journalism, whereby those town-dwellers who cannot go to the country can, by way of solace and refreshment, have the country brought to them, in what may be called the Naturalists' Column of English newspapers. It seems probable that as the desire for a free open-air life is intensified among the prisoners of an artificial commercialism, and as the very excess of our modern "civilisation" necessitates in some measure a return to nature, there will be a corresponding interest in the works of the great poet-naturalists who have heralded this change.

Even now there are many readers, rich and poor alike, who feel and acknowledge a debt of gratitude to Jefferies, not only as the faithful student and historian of English country life, but as the interpreter of Nature's soul. He caught and expressed, as no previous writer had done, the fleeting moods and phenomena of Nature, manifested as clearly in the humblest as in the highest of her works.

> "He showed the soul within
> The veil of matter luminous and thin ;
> He heard the old Earth's undersong piercing the modern din.
>
> "No bird that cleaves the air
> But his revealing thought has made more fair ;
> No tremulous dell of summer leaves but feels his presence there.
>
> "So though we deem him dead,
> Lo ! he yet speaketh ! and the words are sped
> In grassy whispers o'er the fields—by every wildflower said." [1]

---

[1] From the poem on "Richard Jefferies," by Mary Geoghegan, *Temple Bar*, 1892.

That Jefferies' abstruser writings will ever be popular in the ordinary sense, is scarcely to be expected; but they will not on this account have failed of their effect, for by influencing the minds of the finer and more imaginative thinkers—the poets who, as Shelley expressed it, are "the unacknowledged legislators of the world"—his genius will indirectly be a great power in the dissemination of a higher ideal. His personality belongs to that rare order which, in spite of all blemishes and imperfections, can by some subtle magic quicken the sympathies and touch the heart of the reader; it will live and be remembered long after far more showy and pretentious personages are forgotten. "To reflect," he says, "that another human being, if at a distance of ten thousand years, would enjoy one hour's more life, in the sense of fulness of life, in consequence of anything I had done in my little span, would be to me a peace of soul." It is not to be believed that a future and happier society will omit to do honour to the man who wrote these words.

For there are few figures more pathetic or more heroic in the annals of our literature than that of this solitary, unfortunate, yet brave-hearted man, who with "three great giants" against him, as he recorded in his journal, "disease, despair, and poverty," could yet nourish to the last an indomitable confidence in the happiness of the future race. But with the idealist's failure, he had also the idealist's success, in the assurance that thought itself is reality—that to have felt these hopes and aspirations is in the truest

sense to have realised them. In his own words:
"To be beautiful and to be calm, without mental fear, is the ideal of Nature. If I cannot achieve it, at least I can think it."

BIBLIOGRAPHICAL APPENDIX.

I.—WORKS BY JEFFERIES.

EARLY PERIOD, 1872-1878.

1. *Essays.*

* The essays marked with an asterisk have been reprinted in *The Toilers of the Field*, 1892.

"The Wiltshire Labourer," *The Times*, November 14 and 27, 1872.*
Two letters dated from Coate Farm, Swindon. An intermediate letter on "Glebe Allotments" appeared in *The Times*, November 23, 1872. All three are reprinted in *The Toilers of the Field*.
"The Future of Farming," *Fraser's Magazine*, December, 1873.
"John Smith's Shanty," *Fraser's Magazine*, February, 1874.*
"Swindon, its History and Antiquities," *The Wiltshire Archæological and Natural History Magazine*, March, 1884.
"A Railway Accidents Bill," *Fraser's Magazine*, May, 1874.
"The Power of the Farmers," *Fortnightly Review*, June, 1874.
"The Farmer at Home," *Fraser's Magazine*, August, 1874.*
"The Size of Farms," *New Quarterly Magazine*, October, 1874.
"The Labourer's Daily Life," *Fraser's Magazine*, November, 1874.*
"The Shipton Accident," *Fraser's Magazine*, February, 1875.

"Allotment Gardens," *New Quarterly Magazine*, April, 1875.
"The Story of Swindon," *Fraser's Magazine*, May, 1875.
"Field-faring Women," *Fraser's Magazine*, September, 1875.*
"Women in the Field," *Graphic*, September 11, 1875.
"Village Organisation," *New Quarterly Magazine*, October, 1875.
"Twenty Years of Mechanical Farming," *Graphic*, October 23, 1875.
"Village Churches," *Graphic*, December 4, 1875.
"High-pressure Agriculture," *Fraser's Magazine*, August, 1876.
"An English Homestead," *Fraser's Magazine*, November, 1876.*
"Unequal Agriculture," *Fraser's Magazine*, May, 1877.
"The Future of Country Society," *New Quarterly Magazine*, July, 1877.
"A Great Agricultural Problem," *Fraser's Magazine*, March, 1878.

2. *Volumes.*

Reporting, Editing, and Authorship; Practical Hints for Beginners in Literature. John Snow & Co., Ivy Lane; Alfred Bull, Victoria Street, Swindon, 1873, 16mo. Handbook.

Jack Brass, Emperor of England. T. Pettit & Co., 23 Frith Street, Soho, 1873. Pamphlet.

A Memoir of the Goddards of North Wilts. Swindon, 1873, 4to.

The Scarlet Shawl, a novel. Tinsley Brothers, London, 1874. There is said to have been a second edition in 1877.

Restless Human Hearts, a novel. Tinsley Brothers, London, 1875, 3 vols.

Suez-cide; or, How Miss Britannia Bought a Dirty Puddle and Lost Her Sugar Plums. John Snow & Co., Ivy Lane, 1876. A threepenny pamphlet.

World's End, a Story in Three Books. Tinsley Brothers, London, 1877, 3 vols.

Those who are curious in such matters may find in Mr. Besant's *Eulogy of Richard Jefferies*, pp. 145, 146, some account of four boyish romances contributed by Jefferies to the *North Wilts Herald*, in 1866, and entitled respectively, "A Strange Story," "Henrique Beaumont," "Who Will Win? or, American Adventure," and "Masked."

Middle Period, 1878-1880 ("As Naturalist").

The Gamekeeper at Home; or, Sketches from Natural History and Rural Life. Smith & Elder, London, 1878. Reprinted from the *Pall Mall Gazette.* Second edition, 1878. Third edition, 1879. Illustrated by Charles Whymper, 1879, 1890.

Wild Life in a Southern County. Smith & Elder, London, 1879. Reprinted from the *Pall Mall Gazette.* Second edition, 1879. Later editions, 1880, 1889, 1892.

The Amateur Poacher. Smith & Elder, London, 1879. Reprinted from the *Pall Mall Gazette.* Second edition, 1880. New edition, 1893.

Green Ferne Farm, a novel. Smith & Elder, London, 1880.

Hodge and his Masters. Smith & Elder, London, 1880, 2 vols. Reprinted from the *Standard.* New edition, 1 vol., 1890.

Round about a Great Estate. Smith & Elder, London, 1880. Reprinted from the *Pall Mall Gazette.* New edition, 1891.

Later Period, 1881-1887. ("As Poet-Naturalist.")

1. Volumes.

Wood Magic, a Fable. Cassell & Co., London, 1881. 2 vols. Second edition, 1 vol. 1882.
A new edition, Longmans, Green & Co., 1893. Silver Library.

Bevis, the Story of a Boy. Sampson Low & Co., London, 1882. 3 vols. New edition, illustrated, 1 vol. 1891.

The Story of my Heart, my Autobiography. Longmans, Green & Co., London, 1883. Second edition with frontispiece portrait, and preface by C. J. Longman, 1891, in Silver Library.

Nature near London. Chatto & Windus, London, 1883. Essays reprinted from the *Standard.* Later editions, 1883, 1887, 1889, 1891, 1892.

Red Deer. Longmans, Green & Co., London, 1884. New edition, illustrated, 1892, in Silver Library.

The Life of the Fields. Chatto & Windus, London, 1884. Essays reprinted from *Time, Longman's Magazine, The Graphic,*

The Standard, The Magazine of Art, The Gentleman's Magazine, St. James' Gazette, National Review, Manchester Guardian, and *The Pall Mall Gazette.* Later editions, 1888, 1889, 1891, 1892.

The Dewy Morn, a novel. Richard Bentley & Son, London, 1884. 2 vols. New edition, 1 vol. 1891.

After London; or, Wild England. In two parts. Part I., "The Relapse into Barbarism." Part II., "Wild England." Cassell & Co., London, 1885. New edition, 1887.

The Open Air. Chatto & Windus, London, 1885. Essays reprinted from the *Standard, English Illustrated Magazine, Longman's Magazine, St. James' Gazette, Chambers' Journal, Manchester Guardian, Good Words,* and *Pall Mall Gazette.* Later editions, 1888, 1890, 1892.

Amaryllis at the Fair, a novel. Sampson Low & Co., London, 1887.

2. *Contributions by Jefferies to other Books.*

"Out of the Season," a tale by Richard Jefferies, in *The Dove's Nest and Other Stories.* Vizetelly, London, 1886. (The very inferior style of this tale suggests that it was written at a much earlier period.)

Preface by Richard Jefferies to *The Natural History of Selborne,* by Gilbert White. Walter Scott, London, 1887. Pp. 7-12.

POSTHUMOUS VOLUMES.

Field and Hedgerow, being the Last Essays of Richard Jefferies, collected by his Widow. Longmans, Green & Co., London, 1889. Essays reprinted from the *Fortnightly Review, Manchester Guardian, Pall Mall Gazette, Standard, English Illustrated Magazine, Longman's Magazine, St. James' Gazette, Art Journal, Chambers' Journal, Magazine of Art, Cassell's Illustrated Magazine.* There is also included a short poem, "My Chaffinch." There is a large paper edition, with a frontispiece portrait of Jefferies. New edition, small paper, with portrait, in Silver Library.

The Toilers of the Fie'd, with preface by C. J. Longman. Longmans, Green & Co., London, 1892. Part I. consists of six early articles reprinted from *Fraser* and the *Times,* together with a hitherto unprinted essay, "A True Tale of the Wiltshire Labourer"; Part II. of five short papers that appeared in *Longman's Magazine* after Jefferies' death.

There is a large paper edition, with frontispiece portrait, from a photograph of Jefferies' bust in Salisbury Cathedral.

II.—CRITICISM, BIOGRAPHY, &c.

CONTEMPORARY NOTICES.

"The Gamekeeper at Home," *Saturday Review*, August 10, 1878.
"Wild Life," *Saturday Review*, March 1, 1879.
"The Amateur Poacher," *Saturday Review*, November 1, 1879.
"Green Ferne Farm," *Spectator*, March 6, 1880.
"Hodge and his Masters," *Athenæum*, April 10, 1880, by W. E. Henley. *Spectator*, May 29, 1880. *Saturday Review*, June 19, 1880.
"Round about a Great Estate," *Athenæum*, August 14, 1880. *Saturday Review*, August 28, 1880.
"Wood Magic," *Athenæum*, June 4, 1881. *Saturday Review*, July 16, 1881.
"Nature near London," *Athenæum*, May 5, 1883. *Saturday Review*, May 19, 1883.
"The Story of my Heart," *Academy*, November 3, 1883.
"The Life of the Fields," *Saturday Review*, July 12, 1884.
"After London," *Athenæum*, April 11, 1885. *Spectator*, July 4, 1885.
"The Open Air," *Saturday Review*, December 6, 1885.

OBITUARY NOTICES.

Pall Mall Gazette, August 15 and 16, 1887. (The latter of these notices, by Mr. J. W. North, is reprinted in *The Eulogy of Richard Jefferies*, pp. 356-365).
The Athenæum, August 20, 1887.
The Academy, August 20, 1887.

LATER NOTICES.

"Richard Jefferies and the Open Air," *National Review*, October, 1887, by Viscount Lymington.

"The Story of a Heart," *To-day*, June, 1888, by H. S. Salt.

"Richard Jefferies," *Universal Review*, November, 1888, by Edward Garnett.

"The Gospel of Richard Jefferies," *Pall Mall Gazette*, November 16, 1888, by H. S. Salt.

The Eulogy of Richard Jefferies, by Walter Besant. Chatto & Windus, London, 1888, with frontispiece portrait. Second Edition, 1889.

Reviews of *The Eulogy*. *The Academy*, November 17, 1888, by C. E. Dawkins; *Spectator*, November 17, 1888; *Pall Mall Gazette*, November 17, 1888, by H. S. Salt; *The Athenæum*, December 8, 1888, by W. E. Henley; *The Nation* (New York), December 13, 1888.

"Field and Hedgerow," *Saturday Review*, February 9, 1889.

"Richard Jefferies," *The Girl's Own Paper*, August 31, 1889, by Alan Wright.

"Richard Jefferies," *The Girl's Own Paper*, December, 21, 1889, by C. W. M. (Contains the account of Jefferies' alleged conversion.)

Views and Reviews, Essays in Appreciation, by W. E. Henley. David Nutt, London, 1890. "Jefferies," pp. 177-182. (Reprinted from the *Athenæum*.)

"Richard Jefferies," *Scots Observer*, August 2, 1890, by Frederick Greenwood.

"Richard Jefferies," *Murray's Magazine*, Notes of the Month, September, 1890.

"Round about Coate," *Scots Observer*, October 18, 1890, by P. Anderson Graham.

"The Mulberry Tree," a poem by Jefferies, *Scots Observer*, November 8, 1890.

"Richard Jefferies," *Great Thoughts*, December, 1890, with portrait.

"Richard Jefferies" compared with Thoreau, *Life of Henry David Thoreau*, by H. S. Salt. Bentley & Son, London, 1890, pp. 211, 212, 284-286.

Allibone's Critical Dictionary of English Literature, Supplement, 1891; vol. ii., pp, 903, 904. Article on Richard Jefferies.

"Richard Jefferies," *Temple Bar*, June, 1891, by H. S. Salt.

Nature in Books, some Studies in Biography, by P. Anderson Graham. Methuen & Co., London, 1891. Chapter I., "The Magic of the Fields" (Richard Jefferies), pp. 1-43.

"The Pernicious Works of Richard Jefferies," correspondence in *Pall Mall Gazette*, 1891, September, 8, 11, 12, 16, 17, 18, 21.

"Did Richard Jefferies die a Christian? Reminiscences by people who knew him." *Pall Mall Gazette*, September 22, 1891. (Interviews with Mr. Charles Jefferies and "One who knew Jefferies.")

"Did Richard Jefferies die a Christian? an Authoritative Account of the Closing Scene." *Pall Mall Gazette*, October 3, 1891. (Extracts from C. W. M.'s article in *The Girl's Own Paper*.)

"The Conversion of Richard Jefferies," *National Reformer*, October 18, 1891, by H. S. Salt.

"Thoughts on the Labour Question: Passages from Unpublished Chapters by Richard Jefferies," *Pall Mall Gazette*, November 10, 1891.

"Richard Jefferies," *Temple Bar*, January, 1892, a poem by Mary Geoghegan.

"Unveiling the Memorial to Richard Jefferies," *Salisbury and Winchester Journal*, March 12, 1892. (An account of the erection of the bust in Salisbury Cathedral, on March 9, 1892. See also *Saturday Review*, March 12, 1892.)

Dictionary of National Biography, vol. xxix., 1892, "Richard Jefferies," by Richard Garnett, LL.D., pp. 265, 266.

"Homes and Haunts of Richard Jefferies," *Pall Mall Budget*, August 25, 1892 (illustrations).

"Round about Coate," *Art Journal*, January, 1893, by P. Anderson Graham (illustrated).

"Richard Jefferies"; Inlander Leaflets, No. I., reprinted from *The Inlander*, March, 1893, by Dr. S. A. Jones. (*The Inland Press, Ann Arbor*, Michigan, U. S. A.)

PORTRAITS OF RICHARD JEFFERIES.

The only extant photograph of Richard Jefferies is one taken by the London Stereoscopic Company, June 16, 1879, which is pronounced by those who knew him to be an excellent likeness. This photograph is the original from which the various portraits have been reproduced.

The bust by Miss Margaret Thomas, erected in Salisbury Cathedral, March 9, 1892, has been photographed by Mr. Owen of Salisbury, and reproduced in the frontispiece to *Toilers of the Field*, large-paper edition.

THE END.

www.ingramcontent.com/pod-product-compliance
Lightning Source LLC
Chambersburg PA
CBHW031333160426
43196CB00007B/671